W9-BZW-526

UNITY BOOKS

From the Library of

_____

_____

LESSONS IN TRUTH

Also by H. Emilie Cady

Complete Works of H. Emilie Cady
How I Used Truth
God a Present Help (OP)

LESSONS IN TRUTH

H. EMILIE CADY

Unity Classic Library

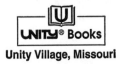

UNITY® Books

Unity Village, Missouri

Lessons in Truth is a member of the Unity Classic Library.

Lessons in Truth was first published in *Unity Magazine* in 1894-95, then published in three paperback volumes in 1896-97. In 1903, the first recorded single volume book was published by Unity School of Christianity now located at 1901 NW Blue Parkway, Unity Village, MO 64065-0001.

To receive a catalog of all Unity publications (books, cassettes, and magazines) or to place an order, call the Customer Service Department: (816) 251-3580 or 1-800-669-0282.

First printing 1903; fiftieth printing 1995

The New Revised Standard Version used for
all Bible verses, unless otherwise noted.

Marbled design by Mimi Schleicher © 1994
Cover design by Jill L. Ziegler

LIBRARY OF CONGRESS CATALOGING-IN-PUBLICATION DATA
Cady, H. Emilie (Harriet Emilie), 1848-1941.
    Lessons in Truth / H. Emilie Cady.
        p.   cm.
    Includes index.
        1. Unity School of Christianity—Doctrines.   I. Title.
BX9890.U505   1995b
289.9'7—dc20   95-6534
ISBN 0-87159-108-1
Canada GST R132529033

Unity Books feels a sacred trust to be a healing presence in the world. By printing with biodegradable soybean ink on recycled paper, we believe we are doing our part to be wise stewards of our Earth's resources.

"You may study with human teachers and from man-made books until doomsday; you may get all the theological lore of the ages; you may understand intellectually all the statements of Truth, and be able to prate healing formulas as glibly as oil flows, but until there is a definite inner revealing of the reality of an indwelling Christ through whom and by whom come life, health, peace, power, *all* things—aye, who *is* all things—you have not yet found "the friendship of the Lord."

H. Emilie Cady

Contents

Lesson

1. Bondage or Liberty, Which? 1

2. Statement of Being 17

3. Thinking 27

4. Denials 43

5. Affirmations 59

6. Faith 71

7. Definition of Terms: Chemicalization,
   Personality, and Individuality......................... 85

8. Spiritual Understanding 97

9. The Secret Place of the Most High 111

10. Finding the Secret Place............................... 125

11. Spiritual Gifts.. 143

12. Unity of the Spirit 157

A Brief Glossary of Truth Terms 171

Index.. 173

About the Author.. 193

BONDAGE OR LIBERTY, WHICH?

First Lesson

[In entering upon this course of instruction, each of you should, so far as possible, lay aside, for the time being, all previous theories and beliefs. By so doing, you will be saved the trouble of trying, all the way through the course, to put "new wine into old wineskins" (Lk. 5:37). If there is anything, as we proceed, that you do not understand or agree with, just let it be passively in your mind until you have read the entire book, for many statements that would at first arouse antagonism and discussion will be clear and easily accepted a little further on. After the course is completed, if you wish to return to your old beliefs and ways of living, you are at perfect liberty to do so. But, for the time being, be willing to become as a little child; for, said a Master in spiritual things, "Unless you ... become like children, you will never enter the kingdom of heaven" (Mt. 18:3). If at times there seems to be repetition, please remember that these are lessons, not lectures.][1]

"Finally, be strong in the Lord and in the strength of his power" (Eph. 6:10).

"Whatever is true, whatever is honorable, whatever is just, whatever is pure, whatever is pleasing, whatever is commendable, if there is any

---

1. This paragraph begins the original *Lessons in Truth* too. However, the material that follows was originally found in the twelfth lesson. We have kept it here because we agree it makes for a better beginning.

excellence and if there is anything worthy of praise, think about these things" (Phil. 4:8).

Every man[2] believes himself to be in bondage to the flesh and to the things of the flesh. All suffering is the result of this belief. The history of the Children of Israel coming out of their long bondage in Egypt is descriptive of the human soul, or consciousness, growing up out of the animal or sense part of man and into the spiritual part.

"Then the Lord said [speaking to Moses], 'I have observed the misery of my people who are in Egypt; I have heard their cry on account of their taskmasters. Indeed, I know their sufferings, and I have come down to deliver them from the Egyptians, and to bring them up out of that land to a good and broad land, a land flowing with milk and honey' " (Ex. 3:7-8).

These words express exactly the attitude of the Creator toward His highest creation, man.

Today, and all the days, He has been saying to us, His children: "I have surely seen the affliction of you who are in Egypt (darkness of ignorance), and have heard your cry by reason of your taskmasters (sickness, sorrow, and poverty); and I am (not I will, but I am now) come down to deliver you out of all this suffering, and to bring you up unto a

2. Throughout this book, out of respect for the author and the historical nature of the writing, we have kept her use of the male noun or pronoun when referring to both women and men.

good land and a large, unto a land flowing with good things" (Ex. 3:7-8 KJV adapted).

It may, or it may not be here in this phase of life, but sometime, somewhere, every human being must come to himself. Having tired of eating husks, he will "get up and go to my father" (Lk. 15:18).

> "For it is written,
>> 'As I live, says the Lord, every knee shall
>> bow to me,
>> and every tongue shall give praise to
>> God.' "

—Romans 14:11

This does not mean that God is a stern autocrat who by reason of supreme power compels man to bow to Him. It is, rather, an expression of the order of divine law, the law of all love, all good. Man, who is at first living in the selfish animal part of himself, will grow up through various stages and by various processes to the divine or spiritual under-standing wherein he knows that he is one with the Father and wherein he is free from all suffering, because he has conscious dominion over all things. Somewhere on this journey the human conscious-ness, or intellect, comes to a place where it gladly bows to its spiritual Self and confesses that this spiritual Self, its Christ, is highest and is Lord. Here and forever after, not with sense of bondage, but with joyful freedom, the heart cries out: "The Lord is king" (Ps. 93:1). Everyone must sooner or later come to this point of experience.

You and I, dear reader, have already come to ourselves. Having become conscious of an oppressive bondage, we have arisen and set out on the journey from Egypt to the land of liberty, and now we cannot turn back if we would. Though possibly there will come times to each of us, before we reach the land of milk and honey (the time of full deliverance out of all our sorrows and troubles), when we shall come into a deep wilderness or against a seemingly impassable Red Sea, when our courage will seem to fail. Yet God says to each one of us, as Moses said to the trembling Children of Israel, "Do not be afraid, stand firm, and see the deliverance that the Lord will accomplish for you today" (Ex. 14:13).

Each man must sooner or later learn to stand alone with his God; nothing else avails. Nothing else will ever make you master of your own destiny. There is in your own indwelling Lord all the life and health, all the strength and peace and joy, all the wisdom and support that you can ever need or desire. No one can give to you as can this indwelling Father. He is the spring of all joy and comfort and power.

Hitherto we have believed that we were helped and comforted by others, that we received joy from outside circumstances and surroundings, but it is not so. All joy and strength and good spring up from a fountain within one's own being, and if we only knew this Truth, we should know that, because *God in us* is the fountain out of which springs all our good, nothing that anyone does or says, or fails to do or say, can take away our joy and good.

Someone has said: "Our liberty comes from an understanding of the mind and the thoughts of God toward us." Does God regard man as His servant or as His child? Most of us have believed ourselves not only the slaves of circumstances, but also, at the best, the *servants* of the Most High. Neither belief is true. It is time for us to awake to right thoughts, to know that we are not servants, but children, "and if children, then heirs" (Rom. 8:17) Heirs to what? Why, heirs to all wisdom, so that we need not, through any lack of wisdom, make mistakes; heirs to all love, so that we need know no fear or envy or jealousy; heirs to all strength, all life, all power, all good.

The human intelligence is so accustomed to the sound of words heard from childhood that often they convey to it no real meaning. Do you stop to think, really to comprehend, what it means to be "heirs of God and joint heirs with Christ" (Rom. 8:17)? It means, as Emerson says, that "every man is the inlet, and may become the outlet, of all there is in God." It means that all that God is and has is in reality for us, His only heirs, if we only know how to claim our inheritance.

This claiming of our rightful inheritance, the inheritance that God wants us to have in our daily life, is just what we are learning how to do in these simple talks.

Paul said truly: "Heirs, as long as they are minors, are no better than slaves, though they are the owners of all the property; but they remain under guardians and trustees until the date set by the father. So with us; while we were minors, we were enslaved to the elemental spirits of the world. But when the fullness of time had come, God sent his Son, born of a woman, born under the law, in order to redeem those who were under the law, so that we might receive adoption as children. And because you are children, God has sent the Spirit of his Son into our hearts, crying, 'Abba! Father!' So you are no longer a slave but a child, and if a child then also an heir, through God" (Gal. 4:1-7).

It is through Christ, the indwelling Christ, that we are to receive all that God has and is, as much or as little as we can or dare to claim.

No matter with what object you first started out to seek Truth, it was in reality because it was God's "fullness of time" (Gal. 4:4) for you to arise and begin to claim your inheritance. You were no longer to be satisfied with or under bondage to the elements of the world. Think of it! God's "fullness of time" *now* for you to be free, to have dominion over all things material, to be no longer bond servant, but a son in possession of your inheritance! "You did not choose me but I chose you. And I appointed you to go and bear fruit" (Jn. 15:16).

We have come to a place now where our search for Truth must no longer be for the rewards; it must no longer be our seeking a creed to follow, but it must be our *living a life*. In these simple lessons, we shall take only the first steps out of the Egyptian bondage of selfishness, lust, and sorrow toward the land of liberty, where perfect love and all good reign.

Every right thought that we think, our every unselfish word or action, is bound by immutable laws to be fraught with good results. But in our walk, we must learn to lose sight of results that are the "loaves and the fish" (Mt. 15:36), we must, rather, seek to be the Truth consciously, to be love, to be wisdom, to be life (as we really are unconsciously), and let results take care of themselves.

Every man must take time daily for quiet and meditation. In daily meditation lies the secret of power. No one can grow in either spiritual knowledge or power without it. Practice the presence of God just as you would practice music. No one would ever dream of becoming a master in music except by spending some time daily alone with music. Daily meditation alone with God focuses the divine Presence within us and brings it to our consciousness.

You may be so busy with the doing, the outgoing of love to help others (which is unselfish and Godlike as far as it goes), that you find no time to go apart. But the command, or rather the invitation, is "come away ... by yourselves and rest a while" (Mk. 6:31). And it is the only way in which you will ever gain definite knowledge, true wisdom, newness of experience, steadiness of purpose, or power to meet the unknown, which must come in all daily life. Doing is secondary to being. When we are consciously the Truth, it will radiate from us and accomplish the works without our ever running to and fro. If you have no time for this quiet meditation, make time, take time. Watch carefully, and you will find that there are some things, even in the active unselfish doing, that would better be left undone than that you should neglect regular meditation.

You will find that some time is spent every day in idle conversation with people who "just run in for a few moments" to be entertained. If you can help such people, well; if not, gather yourself together and do not waste a moment idly diffusing and dissipating yourself to gratify their idleness. You have no idea what you lose by it.

When you withdraw from the world for meditation, let it not be to think of yourself or your failures, but invariably to get all your thoughts centered on God and on your relation to the Creator and Upholder of the universe. Let all the little annoying cares and anxieties go for a while, and by effort, if need be, turn your thoughts away from them to some of the simple words of the Nazarene or of the Psalmist. Think of some Truth statement, be it ever so simple.

No person, unless he has practiced it, can know how it quiets all physical nervousness, all fear, all oversensitiveness, all the little raspings of everyday life—just this hour of calm, quiet waiting alone with God. Never let it be an hour of bondage, but always one of restfulness.

Some, having realized the calm and power that come of daily meditation, have made the mistake of drawing themselves from the world, that they may give their entire time to meditation. This is asceticism, which is neither wise nor profitable.

The Nazarene, who is our noblest type of the perfect life, went daily apart from the world only that he[3] might come again into it with renewed spiritual power. So we go apart into the stillness of divine Presence that we may come forth into the world of everyday life with new inspiration and increased courage and power for activity and for overcoming.

3. In keeping with Cady's original writings, pronoun references to Jesus are not capitalized. For clarity's sake, we have made an exception when the pronoun refers to the inner Christ, in Jesus or us. These pronouns are capitalized.

We talk to God—that is prayer; God talks to us—that is inspiration. We go apart to get still, that new life, new inspiration, new power of thought, new supply from the Fountainhead may flow in; and then we come forth to shed it on those around us, that they, too, may be lifted up. Inharmony cannot remain in any home where even one member of the family daily practices this hour of the presence of God, so surely does the renewed infilling of the heart by peace and harmony result in the continual outgoing of peace and harmony into the entire surroundings.

Again, in this new way that we have undertaken, this living the life of Spirit instead of the old self, we need to seek always to have more and more of the Christ Spirit of meekness and love incorporated into our daily life. Meekness does not mean servility, but it means a spirit that could stand before a Pilate of false accusation and say nothing. No one else is so grand, so godlike as he who, because he knows the Truth of Being, can stand meekly and unperturbed before the false accusations of the human mind. "Thy gentleness hath made me great" (2 Sam. 22:36 KJV).

We must forgive as we would be forgiven. To forgive does not simply mean to arrive at a place of indifference to those who do personal injury to us; it means far more than this. To forgive is to *give for*—to give some actual, definite good in return for evil given. One may say, "I have no one to forgive; I have not a personal enemy in the world." And yet if, under any circumstances, any kind of a "served-him-right" thought springs up within you over anything that any of God's children may do or suffer, you have not yet learned how to forgive.

The very pain that you suffer, the very failure to demonstrate over some matter that touches your own life deeply, may rest upon just this spirit of unforgiveness that you harbor toward the world in general. Put it away with resolution.

Do not be under bondage to false beliefs about your circumstances or environment. God is in everything that happens to you. There are no "second causes." No matter how evil circumstances may appear or how much it may seem that some other personality is at the foundation of your sorrow or trouble, God, good, good alone, is *real* there.

If we have the courage to persist in seeing only God in it all, even "human wrath" (Ps. 76:10) shall be invariably turned to our advantage. Joseph, in speaking of the action of his brethren in selling him into slavery, said, "Even though you intended to do harm to me, God intended it for good" (Gen. 50:20). To them that love God, "all things work together for good for those who love God" (Rom. 8:28), or to them who recognize only God. All things! The very circumstances in your life that seem heartbreaking evils will turn to joy before your very eyes if you will steadfastly refuse to see anything but God in them.

It is perfectly natural for the human mind to seek to escape from its troubles by running away from present environments or by planning some change on the material plane. Such methods of escape are absolutely vain and foolish. "Human help is worthless" (Ps. 60:11).

There is no permanent or real outward way of escape from miseries or circumstances; all help must come from within.

The words *God is my defense and deliverance* held in the silence until they become part of your very being, will deliver you out of the hands and the arguments of the keenest lawyer in the world.

The real inner consciousness that "the Lord is my shepherd, I shall not want" (Ps. 23:1) will supply all wants more surely and far more liberally than can any human hand.

The ultimate aim of every man should be to come into the consciousness of an indwelling God, and then, in all external matters, to affirm deliverance through and by this Divine One. There should not be a running to and fro, making human efforts to aid the Divine, but a calm, restful, unwavering trust in All-Wisdom and All-Power within one as able to accomplish the thing desired.

Victory must be won in the silence of your own being first, and then you need take no part in the outer demonstration of relief from conditions. The very walls of Jericho that keep you from your desire must fall before you.

The Psalmist said:

"I lift up my eyes to the hills
 [or to the Highest One]—
     from where will my help come?
 My help comes from the Lord,
     who made heaven and earth....
 The Lord [your indwelling Lord] will
     keep you from all evil ....
 The Lord will keep your going out and
     your coming in
 from this time on and forevermore."
                    —Psalm 121:1-2, 7-8

Oh, if we could only realize that this mighty Power to save and to protect, to deliver and to make alive, lives forever *within us,* and so cease now and forever looking away to others!

There is but one way to obtain this full realization—the way of the Christ. "I am the way, and the truth, and the life" (Jn. 14:6), spoke the Christ through the lips of the Nazarene.

Your holding to the words *Christ is the way,* when you are perplexed and confused and can see no way of escape, will invariably open a way of complete deliverance.

Study Guide

[Those of you who are joining us in study and prayer are proving the sincerity of your quest for Truth; you are seeking God with your whole heart, and we see you blessed with understanding and abundant good in every area of your life.

If you have never studied *Lessons in Truth* or if you have studied it, perhaps many times, come to this study with an open mind and you will find the import and meaning of each word becoming clearer to you. Each reading will yield greater insight.]

Bible—Deuteronomy 3:22; Psalms 37:9, 125:1-2; Jeremiah 39:18; John 8:32; Romans 8:17

1. The belief that we are in bondage to the flesh and to the things of the flesh is the cause of all

   _____.

2. We are heirs of God. All that God is and has is in reality for us, His only heirs. To what are we heirs? _____

   _____

   _____.

3. No one can grow in either spiritual knowledge or power without _____.

4. Real forgiveness is to *give for*—to give _____

   _____.

5. The very pain that you suffer may be caused by harboring a spirit of _____.

6. The ultimate aim of every person should be to come into the _____.

STATEMENT OF BEING
WHO AND WHAT GOD IS
WHO AND WHAT MAN IS

Second Lesson

When Jesus was talking with the Samaritan woman at the well, he said to her, "God is spirit, and those who worship him must worship in spirit and truth." (John 4:24 ASV reads, "God is a Spirit," but the marginal note is, "God is spirit," and some other versions render this passage, "God is Spirit.") To say "a Spirit" would be to imply the existence of more than one spirit. Jesus, in his statement, did not imply this.

Webster in his definition of spirit says: "An animating or vital principle held to give life to physical organisms. A supernatural being or essence; the Holy Spirit."

God, then, is not, as many of us have been taught to believe, a big personage or man residing somewhere in a beautiful region in the sky, called "heaven," where good people go when they die, and see Him clothed in ineffable glory; nor is He a stern, angry judge only awaiting opportunity somewhere to punish bad people who have failed to live a perfect life here.

God is Spirit, or the creative energy that is the cause of all visible things. God as Spirit is the

invisible life and intelligence underlying all
physical things. There could be no body, or visible part, to anything unless there were first Spirit
as creative cause.

God is not a being or person having life, intelligence, love, power. God is that invisible, intan-
gible, but very real, something we call life. God
is perfect love and infinite power. God is the total
of these, the total of all good, whether manifested
or unexpressed.

There is but one God in the universe, but one
source of all the different forms of life or intelligence that we see, whether they be men, animals,
trees, or rocks.

God is Spirit. We cannot see Spirit with these
fleshly eyes; but when Spirit clothes itself with a
body, when Spirit makes itself visible or manifest
through a material form, then we recognize it.
You do not see the living, thinking "me" when
you look at my body. You see only the form that I
am manifesting.

God is love. We cannot see love, nor grasp any
comprehension of what love is, except as love is
clothed with a form. All the love in the universe
is God. The love between husband and wife,
between parents and children, is just the least little bit of God, as pushed forth through visible
form into manifestation. A mother's love, so infinitely tender, so unfailing, is God's love, only

manifested in greater degree by the mother.

God is wisdom and intelligence. All the wisdom and intelligence that we see in the universe is God—is wisdom projected through a visible form. To educate (from *educare*, to lead forth) never means to force into from the outside but always means to draw out from within something already existing there. God as infinite wisdom lies within every human being, only waiting to be led forth into manifestation. This is true education.

Heretofore we have sought knowledge and help from outside sources, not knowing that the source of all knowledge, the very Spirit of Truth, is lying latent within each one of us, waiting to be called on to teach us the truth about all things—most marvelous of teachers, and everywhere present, without money or price!

God is power. Not simply God has power, but God *is* power. In other words, all the power there is to do anything is God. God, the source of our existence every moment, is not simply omnipotent (all-powerful); He is omnipotence (all power). He is not alone omniscient (all-knowing); He is omniscience (all knowledge). He is not only omnipresent, but more—omnipresence. God is not a being having qualities, but He is the good itself. Everything you can think of that is good, when in its absolute perfection, goes to make up that invisible Being we call God.

God, then, is the substance (from *sub*, under, and *stare*, to stand), or the real thing standing under every visible form of life, love, intelligence, or power. Each rock, tree, animal, every visible thing, is a manifestation of the one Spirit—God—differing only in degree of manifestation; and each of the numberless modes of manifestation or individualities, however insignificant, contains the whole.

One drop of water taken from the ocean is just as perfect ocean water as the whole great body. The constituent elements of water are exactly the same, and they are combined in precisely the same ratio or perfect relation to each other, whether we consider one drop, a pailful, a barrelful, or the entire ocean out of which the lesser quantities are taken; each is complete in itself; they differ only in quantity or degree. Each contains the whole, and yet no one would make the mistake of supposing from this statement that each drop is the entire ocean.

So we say that each individual manifestation of God contains the whole; not for a moment meaning that each individual is God in His entirety, so to speak, but that each is God come forth, shall I say? in different quantity or degree.

Man is the last and highest manifestation of divine energy, the fullest and most complete expression (or pressing out) of God. To man, therefore, is given dominion over all other manifestations.

God is not only the creative cause of every visible form of intelligence and life at its commencement, but each moment throughout its existence, He lives within every created thing as the life, the ever-renewing, re-creating, upbuilding cause of it. He never is and never can be for a moment separated from His creations. Then how can even a sparrow fall to the ground without His knowledge? And "you are of more value than many sparrows" (Mt. 10:31).

God *is*. Man exists (from *ex*, out of, and *sistere*, to stand forth). Man stands forth out of God.

Man is a threefold being, made up of Spirit, soul, and body. Spirit, our innermost, real being, the absolute part of us, the *I* of us, has never changed, though our thoughts and our circumstances may have changed hundreds of times. This part of us is a standing forth of God into visibility. It is the Father in us. At this central part of his being, every person can say, "The Father and I are one" (Jn. 10:30), and speak absolute Truth.

Soul or mortal mind—that which Paul calls "the mind on the flesh" (Rom. 8:6)—is the region of the intellect, where we do conscious thinking. Body is the last or external part of man's being in his descent from God into the material universe.

The great whole of as yet unmanifested Good, or God, from whom we are projections or off-spring, in whom "we live and move and have our being" (Acts 17:28) continually, is to me the Father—*our* Father; "and all ye are brethren" (Mt. 23:8 KJV), because all are manifestations of one and the same Spirit. Jesus, recognizing this, said, "Call no one your father on earth, for you have one Father—the one in heaven" (Mt. 23:9). As soon as we recognize our true relationship to all men, we at once slip out of our narrow, personal loves, our "me and mine," into the universal love that takes in all the world, joyfully exclaiming: " 'Who is my mother, and who are my brothers?' And pointing to his disciples, he said, 'Here are my mother and my brothers!' " (Matt. 12:48-49)

Many have thought of God as a personal being The statement that God is Principle chills them, and in terror, they cry out, "They have taken away my Lord, and I do not know where they have laid him" (Jn. 20:13).

Broader and more learned minds are always cramped by the thought of God as a person, for personality limits to place and time.

God is the name we give to that unchangeable, inexorable principle at the source of all existence To the individual consciousness, God takes on personality, but as the creative underlying cause of all things, He is principle, impersonal. As expressed in each individual, He becomes personal to that one—a personal, loving, all-giving Father-Mother. All that we can ever need or desire is in the infinite Father-Principle, the great reservoir of unexpressed good. There is no limit to the Source of our being, nor to His willingness to manifest more of Himself through us. The only limit is in our knowledge of how to *draw* from the fountain.

Hitherto we have turned our hearts and efforts toward the external for fulfillment of our desires and for satisfaction, and we have been grievously disappointed. The hunger of everyone for satisfaction is only the cry of the homesick child for its Father-Mother God. It is only the Spirit's desire in us to come forth into our consciousness as more and more perfection, until we shall have become *fully* conscious of our oneness with All-Perfection. Man never has been and never can be satisfied with anything less.

We all have direct access through the Father in us—the central "I" of our being—to the great whole of life, love, wisdom, power, which is God. What we now want to know is how to receive more from the Fountainhead and to make more and more of God (which is but another name for All-Good) manifest in our daily lives.

There is but one Source of Being. This Source is the living fountain of all good, be it life, love, wisdom, power—the Giver of all good gifts. This Source and you are connected, every moment of your existence. You have power to draw on this Source for all of good you are, or ever will be, capable of desiring.

Study Guide

Bible—Jeremiah 23:23-24; Zephaniah 3:17; Matthew 23:9; John 4:24

1. God is not a being or person having life, intelligence, love, and power. He *is* life, intelligence, love, and power; He is the total of _____.

2. Man is the most complete expression of ____.

3. Man is a threefold being, made up of_____, _____, and_____.

4. Soul or mortal mind is the region of the intellect where we do _____.

5. God is both impersonal (principle) and personal. As the _____, He is principle, impersonal. As expressed in each individual, He becomes_____.

THINKING

Third Lesson

We learned in the second lesson that the real substance within everything we see is God, that all things are one and the same Spirit in different degrees of manifestation, that all the various forms of life are just the same as one life come forth out of the invisible into visible forms, that all the intelligence and all the wisdom in the world are God as wisdom in various degrees of manifestation, that all the love that people feel and express toward others is just a little, so to speak, of God as love come into visibility through the human form.

When we say there is but one Mind in the entire universe, and that this Mind is God, some persons, having followed understandingly the second lesson and recognized God as the one Life, one Spirit, one Power, pushing Himself out into various degrees of manifestation through people and things, will at once say, "Yes, that is all plain."

But someone else will say, "If all the mind there is, is God, then how can I think wrong thoughts or have any but God thoughts?"

The connection between universal Mind and our own individual minds is one of the most difficult things to put into words, but when it once dawns on one, it is easily seen.

There is in reality only one Mind (or Spirit, which is life, intelligence, and so forth) in the universe; and yet there is a sense in which we are individual, or separate, a sense in which we are free wills and not puppets.

Man is made up of Spirit, soul, and body. Spirit is the central unchanging "I" of us, the part that since infancy has never changed, and to all eternity never will change. Soul, or what metaphysical Christians call "mortal mind," is the region of the intellect where we do conscious thinking and are free wills. This part of our being is in constant process of changing.

In our outspringing from God into the material world, Spirit is inner—one with God; soul or mortal mind or intellect is the clothing, as it were, of the Spirit; body is the external clothing of the soul. Yet all are in reality one, the composite man—as steam, water, and ice are one, only in different degrees of condensation. In thinking of ourselves, we must not separate Spirit, soul, and body, but rather hold all as one, if we would be strong and powerful. Man originally lived consciously in the spiritual part of himself. He fell by descending in his consciousness to the external or more material part of himself.

Mortal mind, the term so much used and so distracting to many, is the intellect, which gathers its information from the outside world through the five senses. This mortal mind has no way of knowing truth from falsehood. It is what Paul calls "the mind on the flesh" in contradistinction to spiritual mind, and he flatly says: "The mind on the flesh [believing what the carnal mind says] is death [sorrow, trouble, sickness], but to set the mind on the Spirit [ability to still the carnal mind and let the Spirit speak within us] is life and peace" (Rom. 8:6).

The Spirit within you is Divine Mind, the *real* mind. Without it, the human mind would disappear, just as a shadow disappears when the real thing that casts it is removed. Man then, is Spiritual Mind, mortal mind, and body.

If you find this subject of human mind and universal Mind puzzling to you, do not worry over it. Just drop it for a time, and as you go on with the lessons, you will find that some day an understanding of it will flash suddenly upon you with perfect clearness.

There are today two classes of people, so far as mentality goes, who are seeking deliverance out of sickness, trouble, and unhappiness, by spiritual means. One class requires that every statement made be proved by the most elaborate and logical argument before it can or will be received. The other class is willing at once to "become like children" (Mt. 18:3) and just be taught how to take the first steps toward pure understanding (or knowledge of Truth as God sees it), and then receives the light by direct revelation from the All-Good. Both are seeking and eventually both will reach the same goal, and neither one should be unduly condemned.

If you are one who seeks and expects to get any realizing knowledge of spiritual things through argument or reasoning, no matter how scholarly your attainments or how great you are in worldly wisdom, you are a failure in spiritual understanding. You are attempting an utter impossibility—that of crowding the Infinite into the quart measure of your own intellectual capacity.

"Those who are unspiritual do not receive the gifts of God's Spirit, for they are foolishness to them, and they are unable to understand them because they are spiritually discerned" (1 Cor. 2:14). Eventually you will find that you are only beating around on the outside of the "kingdom of heaven," though in close proximity to it, and you will then become willing to let your intellect take the place of the child, without which no man can enter in.

" 'No eye has seen, nor ear heard, nor the human heart conceived, what God has [not *will*] prepared for those who love him'—these things God has revealed to us through the Spirit.... For what human being knows what is truly human except the human spirit that is within? So also no one comprehends what is truly God's except the Spirit of God" (I Cor. 2:9-11).

For all those who must wade through months and perhaps years of this purely intellectual or mental process, there are today many books to help and many teachers of metaphysics who are doing noble and praiseworthy work in piloting these earnest seekers after Truth and satisfaction. To them we cry: "All speed!"

But we believe with Paul that "God's foolishness is wiser than human" (1 Cor. 1:25) and that each man has direct access to all there is in God. We are writing for the "children" who, without question or discussion, are willing at once to accept and to try a few plain, simple rules, such as Jesus taught the common people, who "heard him gladly" (Mk. 6:20 KJV)—rules by which they can find the Christ (or the Divine) within themselves, that through it, each man for himself may work out his own salvation from all his troubles.

In other words, there is a shortcut to the top of the hill. While there is a good but long roundabout road for those who need it, we prefer the less laborious means of attaining the same end—by seeking directly the Spirit of Truth promised to dwell *in* us and to lead us into all Truth. My advice: If you want to make rapid progress in growth toward spiritual understanding, stop reading many books. They only give you someone's opinion about Truth or a sort of history of the author's experience in seeking Truth. What you want is revelation of Truth in your own soul, and that will never come through the reading of many books.

Seek light from the Spirit of Truth within you. Go alone. Think alone. Seek light alone, and if it does not come at once, do not be discouraged and run off to someone else to get light; for, as we said before, by so doing, you get only the opinion of the intellect, and may be then further away from the Truth you are seeking than ever before; for the mortal mind may make false reports.

The very Spirit of Truth is at your call, within you. "The anointing that you received from him abides in you" (I Jn. 2:27). Seek it. Wait patiently for it to "guide you into all the truth" (Jn. 16:13) about all things.

"Let the same mind be in you that was in Christ Jesus" (Phil. 2:5). This is the universal Mind, which makes no mistakes. Still the intellect for the time being, and let universal Mind speak to you. When it speaks, though it be but "a still small voice" (1 Kings 19:12 KJV), you will know that what it says is Truth.

How will you know? You will know just as you know that you are alive. All the argument in the world to convince you against Truth that comes to you through direct revelation will fall flat and harmless at your side. And the Truth that you know, not simply believe, you can use to help others. That which comes forth through your spirit will reach the very innermost spirit of him to whom you speak.

What is born from the outside, or intellectual perception, reaches only the intellect of him you would help.

The intellect that is servant to the real Mind, and when servant (but not when master) is good, loves to argue; but when its information is based on the evidence of the senses and not on the true thoughts of the Divine Mind, it is very fallible and full of error.

Intellect argues. Spirit takes the deep things of God and reveals Truth to man. One may be true; the other always is true. Spirit does not give opinions about Truth; it is Truth, and it reveals itself.

Someone has truly said that the merest child who has learned from the depths of his being to say, "Our Father," is infinitely greater than the most intellectual man who has not yet learned it. Paul was a man of gigantic intellect, learned in all the law, a Pharisee of the Pharisees; but after he was spiritually illumined, he wrote, "For God's foolishness is wiser than human wisdom, and God's weakness is stronger than human strength" (I Cor. 1:25).

It does make a great difference in our daily lives what we think about God, about ourselves, about our neighbors. Heretofore, through ignorance of our real Self and of the results of our thinking, we have let our thoughts flow at random. Our minds have been turned toward the external of our being, our body, and nearly all our information has been gotten through our five senses. We have thought wrong because we have been misinformed by these senses, and our troubles and sorrows are the results of our wrong thinking.

"But," says someone, "I do not see how my thinking evil or wrong thoughts about God, or about anyone, can make me sick or my husband lose his position."

Well, I will not just now try to explain all the steps by which bad results follow false thinking, but I will just ask you to try thinking true, right thoughts awhile and see what the results will be.

Take the thought "God loves me" and think the words over and over continually for a few days, trying to realize that they are true, and see what the effect will be on your body and circumstances.

First, you get a new exhilaration of mind, with a great desire and a sense of power to please God; then a quicker, better circulation of blood, with sense of a pleasant warmth in the body, followed by better digestion. Later, as Truth flows out through your being into your surroundings, everybody will begin to manifest a new love for you without your knowing why; and finally, circumstances will begin to change and fall into harmony with your desires, instead of being adverse to them.

Everyone knows how strong thoughts of fear or grief have turned hair white in a few hours, how great fear makes the heart beat so rapidly as to seem about to "jump out of the body"; this result not being at all dependent on whether there be any real cause of fear or whether it be a purely imaginary cause. Just so, strong negative thoughts may render the blood acid, causing rheumatism. Bearing mental burdens makes more stooped shoulders than does bearing heavy material loads. Believing that God regards us as "miserable sinners," that He is continually watching us and our failures with disapproval, brings utter discouragement and a sort of half-paralyzed condition of mind and body, which means failure in all our undertakings.

Is it difficult for you to understand why, if God lives in us all the time, He does not keep our thoughts right instead of permitting us through ignorance to drift into wrong thoughts and so bring trouble on ourselves?

Well, we are not automatons. Your child will never learn to walk alone if you always do his walking. Because you recognize that the only way for him to be strong, self-reliant in all things—in other words, to become a man—is to throw him on himself and let him, through *experience*, come to a knowledge of things for himself; you are not willing to make a mere puppet of him by taking the steps for him, even though you know that he will fall down many times and give himself severe bumps in his ongoing toward perfect physical manhood.

We are in the process of growth into the highest spiritual manhood and womanhood. We get many falls and bumps on the way, but only through these, not necessarily *by* them, can our growth proceed. Father and mother, no matter how strong or deep their love, cannot grow for their children; nor can God, who is Omnipotence, at the center of our being, grow spiritually for us without making of us automatons instead of individuals.

If you keep your thoughts turned toward the external of yourself or of others, you will see only the things that are not real, but temporal, and that pass away. All the faults, failures, or lacks in people or circumstances will seem very real to you, and you will be unhappy and sick.

If you turn your thoughts away from the external toward the spiritual and let them dwell on the good in yourself and in others, all the apparent evil will first drop out of your thoughts and then out of your life. Paul understood this when he wrote to the Philippians: "Finally, beloved, whatever is true, whatever is honorable, whatever is just, whatever is pure, whatever is pleasing, whatever is commendable, if there is any excellence and if there is anything worthy of praise, think about these things" (Phil. 4:8).

We all can learn how to turn the conscious mind toward universal Mind, or Spirit, within us. We can, by practice, learn how to make this everyday, topsy-turvy "mind on the flesh" be still and let the mind that is God (All-Wisdom, All-Love) think in us and out through us.

Imagine, if you will, a great reservoir out of which lead innumerable small rivulets or channels. At its farther end, each channel opens out into a small fountain. This fountain is not only being continually filled and replenished from the reservoir but is itself a radiating center, whence it gives out in all directions that which it receives so that all who come within its radius are refreshed and blessed.

This is our relation to God. Each one of us is a radiating center. Each one, no matter how small or ignorant, is the little fountain at the far end of a channel, the other end of which leads out from all there is in God. This fountain represents our free will or individuality, as separate from the Great Reservoir—God—and yet as one with Him in that we are constantly fed and renewed from Him, and without Him we are nothing.

Each of us, no matter how insignificant he may be in the world, may receive from God unlimited good of whatever kind he desires and radiate it to all about him. But remember, he must radiate if he would receive more. Stagnation is death.

Oh, I want the simplest mind to grasp the idea that the very wisdom of God—the love, the life, and the power of God are ready and waiting with longing impulse to flow out through us in unlimited degree! When it flows in unusual degree through the intellect of a certain person, men exclaim, "What a wonderful mind!" When it flows through the hearts of men, it is the love that melts all bitterness, envy, selfishness, jealousy, before it. When it flows through their bodies as life, no disease can withstand its onward march.

We do not have to beseech God any more than we have to beseech the sun to shine. The sun shines because it is a law of its being to shine, and it cannot help it. No more can God help pouring into us unlimited wisdom, life, power, all good, because to give is a law of His being. Nothing can hinder Him except our own lack of understanding. The sun may shine ever so brightly, but if we have, through willfulness or ignorance, placed ourselves, or have been placed by our progenitors, in the far corner of a damp, dark cellar, we get neither joy nor comfort from its shining; then to us the sun never shines.

So we have heretofore known nothing of how to get ourselves out of the cellar of ignorance, doubt, and despair; to our wrong thinking, God has seemed to withhold the life, wisdom, power, we wanted so much, though we sought Him ever so earnestly.

The sun does not radiate life and warmth today and darkness and chill tomorrow; it cannot, from the nature of its being. Nor does God radiate love at one time, while at other times, anger, wrath, and displeasure flow from His mind toward us.

"Does a spring pour forth from the same opening both fresh and brackish water? Can a fig tree, my brothers and sisters, yield olives, or a grapevine figs?" (Jas. 3:11-12)

God is All-Good—always good, always love. He never changes, no matter what we do or may have done. He is always trying to pour more of Himself through us into visibility so as to make us grander, larger, fuller, freer individuals.

While the child is crying out for its Father-Mother God, the Father-Mother is yearning with infinite tenderness to satisfy the child.

> In the heart of man a cry,
> In the heart of God, supply.

SUMMARY

1. There is but one Mind in the universe.

2. Mortal mind is human mind or intellect. It gathers its information and finds its authority from *without*; Universal Mind sees and speaks from *within*.

3. Intellect is the servant of Spirit. Body is the servant of intellect.

4. Our ways of thinking make our happiness or unhappiness, our success or nonsuccess. We can, by effort, change our ways of thinking.

5. God is at all times, regardless of our so-called sins, trying to pour more good into our lives to make them richer and more successful.

Study Guide

Bible—Philippians 2:5, 4:8; 1 Corinthians 1:25

1. There is in reality only one Mind. Yet, there appears to be more than one Mind because we are _____.

2. Man is made up of Spirit, soul, and body. Spirit is_____; soul is_____ _____; body is _____.

3. Troubles and sorrows are the results of our wrong thinking. We have thought wrong because we have been misinformed by our ___ _____.

4. God doesn't force us to think and act aright because this would make us _____ instead of _____.

5. If we are to receive more of God's unlimited good, we must _____.

DENIALS

Fourth Lesson

"Then Jesus told his disciples, 'If any want to become my followers, let them deny themselves and take up their cross and follow me.' "

—Matthew 16:24

Al systems for spiritualizing the mind include denial.[1] Every religion in all the ages had some sort of denial as one of its foundations.

We all know how the Puritans believed that the more rigidly they denied themselves comfort, the better they pleased God. So far has this idea taken possession of the human mind during some ages that devout souls have even tortured their bodies in various ways, believing that they were thus making themselves more spiritual, or at least were in some way placating an angry God. Even today many interpret the above quoted saying of Jesus as meaning: If any man wants to please God, he must give up about all the enjoyment and comfort he has, all

1. In today's usage, the psychological meaning of *denial*, that of refusing to face up to the truth, so predominates that use of this term causes considerable confusion. Whether to accept the reality of something or to deny it is an issue of great delicacy and the reader is encouraged to proceed prayerfully. It seems important to acknowledge the appearance of a circumstance but deny its power over us.

things he likes and wants, and must take up the heavy cross of constantly doing the things that are repugnant to him in his daily life. This is why many young people say, "When I am old, I will be a Christian, but not now, for I want to enjoy life awhile first."

There could, I am sure, be nothing further from the meaning of the Nazarene than the foregoing interpretation. In our ignorance of the nature of God, our Father, and of our relation to Him, we have believed that all our enjoyment came from external sources, usually from gaining possession of something we did not have. The poor see enjoyment only in possessing abundance of money. The rich, who are satiated with life's so-called pleasures until their lives have become like a person with an overloaded stomach, compelled to sit constantly at a well-spread table, are often the most bitter in the complaint that life holds no happiness for them. The sick one believes that, were he well, he would be perfectly happy. The healthy but hardworking person feels the need of some days of rest and recreation, that the monotony of his life may be broken.

So ever the mind has been turned to some external change of condition or circumstance in pursuit of satisfaction and enjoyment. In after years, when men have tried all, getting first this thing and then that which they thought would yield them happiness and have been grievously disappointed; in a kind of desperation, they turn to God and try to find some sort of comfort in believing that sometime, somewhere, they will get what they want and be happy. Thenceforth their lives are patient and submissive, but they are destitute of any real joy.

This same Nazarene, to whom we always return because to us he is the best-known teacher and demonstrator of Truth, spent nearly three years teaching the people—the common everyday people like you and me, who wanted, just as we do, food and rent and clothing, money, friends, and love— to love their enemies and to do good to those who persecuted them, to resist not evil in any way but to give double to anyone who tried to get what belonged to them, to cease from all anxiety regarding the things they needed because "your heavenly Father knows that you need all these things" (Mt. 6:32).

And then in talking one day, he said, "I have said these things to you so that my joy may be in you, and that your joy may be complete" (Jn. 15:11). And he continued, "The Father will give you whatever you ask him in my name" (Jn. 15:16). "Ask and you will receive, so that your joy may be complete.... I do not say to you that I will ask the Father on your behalf; for the Father himself loves you" (Jn. 16:24, 26-27). We have further learned that God is the total of all the good in the universe and that there is in the mind which is God a perpetual desire to pour more of Himself—the substance of all good things—through us into visibility, or into our lives.

Surely all these things do not make it look as though, when Jesus said that the way to be like him and to possess a like power was to *deny* oneself, he meant that we are not to go without the enjoyable comforts of life or in any way deprive or torture ourselves.

In these lessons, we have seen that besides the real innermost Self of each of us—the Self that is the divine Self because it is an expression or pressing out of God into visibility and is always one with the Father—there is a human self, a carnal mind, that reports lies from the external world and is not to be relied upon fully; this is the self of which Jesus spoke when he said, "let them deny themselves" (Mt. 16:24). This intellectual man, carnal mind, or whatever you choose to call him, is envious and jealous and fretful and sick because he is selfish. The human self seeks its own gratification at the expense, if need be, of someone else.

Your divine Self is never sick, never afraid, never selfish. It is the part of you that "does not insist on its own way; it is not irritable or resentful" (1 Cor. 13:5). It is always seeking to give to others, while the human self is always seeking its own. Heretofore we have lived more in the human region. We have believed all that the carnal mind has told us, and the consequence is that we have been overwhelmed with all kinds of privation and suffering.

Some people who, during the last few years, have been making a special study of the mind find it a fact that certain wrong or false beliefs held by us are really the cause of all sorts of trouble—physical, moral, and financial. They have learned that wrong (or, as they call them, *error*) beliefs arise only in the human mind. They have learned and actually proved that we can, by a persistent effort of the will, change our beliefs, and by this means alone, entirely change our troublesome circumstances and bodily conditions.

One of the methods that they have found will work every time in getting rid of troublesome conditions (which are all the result of erroneous thinking and feeling) is to deny them *in toto*: First, to deny that any such things have, or could have, power to make us unhappy; second, to deny that these things do in *reality*[2] exist at all.

The word *deny* has two definitions, according to *Webster*. To deny, in one sense, is "to refuse to grant," as to deny bread to the hungry. To deny, in another sense (and we believe it was in this latter way that Jesus used it) is "to declare untrue," to repudiate as utterly false. To deny oneself, then, is

2. Reality in the Absolute, not the relative reality we live in daily.

not to withhold comfort or happiness from the external man, much less to inflict torture upon him, but it is to deny the claims of error consciousness, to declare these claims to be untrue.

If you have done any piece of work incorrectly, the very first step toward getting it right is to undo the wrong and begin again from that point. We have believed wrong about God and about ourselves. We have believed that God was angry with us and that we were sinners who ought to be afraid of Him. We have believed that sickness and poverty and other troubles are evil things put here by this same God to torture us in some way into serving Him and loving Him. We have believed that we have pleased God best when we have become so absolutely subdued by our troubles as to be patiently submissive to them all, not even trying to rise out of them or to overcome them. All this is false, entirely false! And the first step toward freeing ourselves from our troubles is to get rid of our erroneous beliefs about God and about ourselves.

"But," objects one, "if a thing is not true and I have believed a lie about it, I do not see just how my believing wrong about it could affect my bodily health or my circumstances."

A child can be so afraid of an imaginary bugaboo under the bed as to have convulsions. Should you, today, receive a telegraphic message that your husband, wife, or child, who is absent from you, had been suddenly killed, your suffering, mental and physical, and perhaps extending even to your external and financial affairs, would be just as great as though the report really were true, and yet it might be entirely false. Exactly so have these messages of bugaboos behind the doors, bugaboos of divine wrath and of our own weakness, come to us through the senses until we are overcome by our fears of them.

Now, let us arouse ourselves. Denial is the first practical step toward wiping out of our minds the mistaken beliefs of a lifetime—the beliefs that have made such sad havoc in our lives. By denial, we mean declaring not to be true a thing that seems true. Negative appearances are directly opposed to the teachings of Truth. Jesus said, "Do not judge by appearances, but judge with right judgment" (Jn. 7:24).

Suppose you had always been taught that the sun really moved or revolved around the earth, and someone should now try to persuade you that the opposite is the truth: you would see at once that such might be the case, and yet as often as you saw the sun rise, the old impression, made on your mind by the wrong belief of years, would come up and seem almost too real to be disputed. The only way by which you could cleanse your mind of the impression and make the untrue seem unreal would be by repeatedly denying the old beliefs, saying over and over to yourself as often as the subject came up in your mind: "This is not true. The sun does not move; it stands still, and the earth moves." Eventually the sun would only seem to move.

The appearances are that our bodies and our circumstances control our thoughts, but the opposite is true. Our thoughts control our bodies and our circumstances.

If you repeatedly deny a false or unhappy condition, it loses its power to make you unhappy.

What everyone desires is to have only the good manifested in his life and surroundings—to have his life full of love, to have perfect health, to know all things, to have great power and much joy—and this is just exactly what God wants us to have. All love is God in manifestation, as we have learned in a previous lesson. All wisdom is God. All life and health are God. All joy (because all good) and all power are God. All good of whatever kind is God come forth into visibility through people or some other visible form. When we crave more of any good thing, we are in reality craving more of God to come forth into our lives so that we can realize it by the senses. Having more of God does not take out of our lives the good things—it only puts more of them in. In the mind that is God, there is always the desire to give more, for the divine plan is forever to get more good into visibility.

Intellectually we may see the fact of our own

God-being, which never changes. What we need is to realize our oneness with the Father at all times. In order to realize it, we deny in ourselves and others the appearances that seem contrary to this— deny them as realities; we declare that they are not true.

There are four common error thoughts to which nearly everyone grants great power. Persons who have grown out of sickness and trouble through prayer have found it good to deny these thoughts in order to cleanse the mind of the direful effects of believing them. They can be denied like this:

First: *There is no evil.*

There is but one power in the universe, and that is God—Good. God is good, and God is omnipresence. Apparent evils are not entities or things of themselves. They are simply apparent absence of the good, just as darkness is an absence of light. But God, or good, is omnipresent, so the apparent absence of good (evil) is unreal. It is only an appearance of evil, just as the moving sun was an appearance. You need not wait to discuss this matter of evil or to understand fully all about why you deny it, but begin to practice the denials in an unprejudiced way and see how marvelously they will, after a while, deliver you from some of the so-called evils of your daily life.

Second: *There is no absence of life, substance, or intelligence anywhere.*

We have seen that the real is the spiritual. "What can be seen is temporary, but what cannot be seen is eternal" (2 Cor. 4:18). By using this denial, you will soon break your bondage to matter and to material conditions. You will know that you are free.

Third: *Pain, sickness, poverty, old age, and death cannot master me, for they are not real.*

Fourth: *There is nothing in all the universe for me to fear, for greater is He that is within me than he that is in the world.*

God says, "I will contend with those who contend with you" (Is. 49:25). He says it to every living child of His, and every person is His child.

Repeat these four denials silently several times a day, not with a strained anxiety to get something out of them, but trying calmly to realize the meaning of the words spoken:

There is no evil (or devil).

There is no absence of life, substance, or intelligence anywhere.

Pain, sickness, poverty, old age, and death cannot master me, for they are not real.

There is nothing in all the universe for me to fear,

for greater is He that is within me than he that is in the world.

Almost hourly little vexations and fears come up in your life. Meet each one with a denial. Calmly and coolly say within yourself, "That's nothing at all. It cannot harm or disturb me or make me unhappy." Do not fight it vigorously but let your denial be the denial of any thought of its superiority over you, as you would deny the power of ants on their little hill to disturb you. If you are angry, stand still and silently deny it. Say that you are not angry, that you are love made manifest and cannot be angry, and the anger will leave you.

If someone shows you ill will, silently deny his power to hurt you or to make you unhappy. Should you find yourself feeling jealous or envious toward anyone, instantly turn the heel of denial on the hydra-headed monsters. Declare that you are not jealous or envious, that you are an expression of perfect love (an expression which is God pressed out into visibility) and cannot feel negation. There is really no reason for jealousy or envy, for all persons are one and the same Spirit. "And there are varieties of activities [or manifestations], but it is the same God who activates all of them in everyone" (1 Cor. 12:6), says Paul. How can you be envious of a part of yourself that seems to you more comely?

Shall the foot be envious of the hand, or the ear

of the eye? Are not the seemingly feeble members of the body just as important to the perfection of the whole as the others? Do you seem to be less, or to have less, than some others? Remember that all envy and all jealousy are in the human or mortal mind and that in reality you, however insignificant, are an absolute necessity to God in order to make the perfect whole.

If you find yourself dreading to meet anyone, or afraid to step out and do what you want or ought to do, immediately begin to say, "It is not true; I am not afraid; I am perfect love and can know no fear. No one, nothing in all the universe, can hurt me." You will find after a little that all the fear has disappeared, all trepidation has gone.

Denial brings freedom from bondage, and happiness comes when we can effectually deny the power of anything to touch or to trouble us.

Have you been living in negation for years, denying your ability to succeed, denying your health, denying your Godhood, denying your power to accomplish anything, by feeling yourself a child of the devil or of weakness? If so, this constant negation has paralyzed you and weakened your power.

When, in the next lesson, you learn something about affirmations, the opposite of denials, you will know how to lift yourself out of the realm of failure into that of success.

All your happiness, all your health and power,

come from God. They flow in an unbroken stream from the Fountainhead into the very center of your being and radiate from center to circumference. When you acknowledge this constantly and deny that outside things can hinder your happiness or health or power, it helps you to realize health and power and happiness.

No person or thing in the universe, no chain of circumstances, can by any possibility interpose itself between you and all joy—all good. You may think that something stands between you and your heart's desire, and so live with that desire unfulfilled, but it is not true. This "thing" is the bugaboo under the bed that has no reality. Deny it, deny it, and you will find yourself free, and you will realize that this seeming was all false. Then you will see the good flowing into you, and you will see clearly that nothing can stand between you and your own.

Denials may be spoken silently or audibly, but not in a manner to call forth antagonism and discussion.

To some, all this sort of mechanical working will seem a strange way of entering into a more spiritual life. There are those who easily and naturally glide out of the old material life into a deeper spiritual one without any external help, but there are thousands of others who are seeking primarily "the loaves and fish" of bodily health and financial success, but who, without knowing it, really are seeking a higher way of life, who must take these very first steps. For such, the practicing of these mechanical steps in a wholehearted way, without prejudice, is doing the very best thing possible toward attaining purity of heart and life, toward growth in divine knowledge and fullness of joy in all things undertaken.

Study Guide

Bible—Joel 3:10; Zephaniah 3:15; Matthew 6:8-11, 16:24; Luke 9:23; John 7:24

1. When Jesus said they must "deny themselves," he was not teaching denial of the comforts of life. He was teaching to deny the claims of____

   _____.

2. Jesus said, "Do not judge by appearances, but judge with right judgment." By denial, we mean declaring not to be true a thing that ____

   _____.

3. Four great denials are: (1) _____,
   (2) _____
   _____, (3) _____
   _____, (4) ____
   _____.

4. There is no evil, because_____
   _____.

AFFIRMATIONS

Fifth Lesson

"You will pray to him, and he will hear you,
     and you will pay your vows.
You will decide on a matter, and it will be
     established for you,
     and light will shine on your ways."
                                        —Job 22:27-28

Most people, when they first consciously set out to gain a fuller, higher knowledge of spiritual things, do so because of dissatisfaction—or perhaps unsatisfaction would be the better word—with their present conditions of life. Inherent in the human mind is the thought that somewhere, somehow, it ought to be able to bring to itself that which it desires and which would satisfy. This thought is but the foreshadowing of that which really is.

Our wishes, it is said, do measure just
     Our capabilities. Who with his might
Aspires unto the mountain's upper height,
     Holds in that aspiration a great trust
     To be fulfilled, a warrant that he must
Not disregard, a strength to reach the height
To which his hopes have taken flight.
                                        —Author Unknown

The hunger that we feel is but the prompting of the Divine within us, which longs with an infinite longing to fill us. It is but one side of the law of demand and supply, the other side of which is unchangeably, unfailingly, the promise: "Whatever you ask for in prayer, believe that you have received it, and it will be yours" (Mk. 11:24). The supply is always equal to the demand, but there must first be a demand before supply is of use.

There is, attainable by us, a place where we can see that our doing can cease, because we realize that Spirit is the fulfillment of all of our desires. We simply get still and know that all things whatever we desire are ours already, and this knowing it, or recognizing it, has power to bring the invisible God (or good)—the innermost substance of all things— forth into just the visible form of good that we want.

But in order to attain this place of power, we must take the preliminary steps, faithfully, earnestly, trustingly, though these steps at first glance seem to us as useless and as empty as do the ceremonial forms and religious observances of the ritualistic churchman.

To affirm anything is to assert positively that it is so, even in the face of all contrary evidence. We may not be able to see *how*, by our simply affirming a thing to be true, a thing that to all human reasoning or sight does not seem to be true at all, that we can bring this thing to pass; but we can compel ourselves to cease all futile quibbling and go to work to prove the rule, each one in his own life.

The beautiful Presence all about us and within us is the substance of every good that we can possibly desire—aye, infinitely more than we are capable of desiring, for "no eye has seen, nor ear heard, nor the human heart conceived, what God has prepared for those who love him" (1 Cor. 2:9).

In some way, which it is not easy to put into words—for spiritual laws cannot always be compassed in words, and yet they are none the less infallible, immutable laws that work with precision and certainty—there is power in our word of faith to bring all good things right into our everyday life.

We speak the word, we confidently affirm, but we have nothing to do with the "establishing" of the word, or bringing it to pass. "You will decide on a matter, and it will be established for you" (Job 22:28). So if we decree or affirm unwaveringly, steadfastly, we hold God by His own unalterable laws to do the establishing or fulfilling.

They who have carefully studied spiritual laws find that, besides denying the reality and power of apparent evil, which denying frees them from it, they also can bring any desired good into their lives by persistently affirming it is there already. In the first instructions given to students, the denials and affirmations take a large place. Later on, their own personal experiences and inward guidance lead them up to a higher plane where they no longer need rote repetitions.

The saying over and over of any denial or affirmation is a necessary self-training of a mind that has lived so long in error and false belief that it needs this constant repetition of Truth to unclothe it and to clothe it anew.

As it is with the denials, so with the affirmations. There are four sweeping affirmations of Truth that cover a multitude of lesser ones, and which do marvelous work in bringing good to ourselves and to others.

First: *God is life, love, intelligence, substance, omnipotence, omniscience, omnipresence.*

These ideas you learned in the second lesson—"Statement of Being." As you repeat the affirmation, please remember that every particle of life, love, intelligence, power, or of real substance in the universe is simply a certain degree, or so to speak, a *quantity* of God made manifest or visible through a form. Try to think what it means when you say that God is omnipresent, omnipotent, omniscient.

If God is omnipresence (All-Presence) and All-Good, where is the evil? If He is omnipotence (All-Power), what other power can there be working in the universe?

Since God is omnipotence and omnipresence, put aside forever your traditional teaching of an adverse power, evil (devil), that may at any moment thwart the plans of God and bring you harm.

Do not disturb yourself about the *appearance* of evil all about you, but in the very presence of what seems evil stand true and unwavering in affirming that God, the good, is omnipresence. By so doing, you will see the seeming evil melt away as the darkness before the light or as the dew before the morning sun, and good come to take its place.

Second: *I am a child or manifestation of God, and every moment His life, love, wisdom, power flow into and through me. I am one with God and am governed by His law.*

Remember while repeating this affirmation that nothing—no circumstance, no person or set of persons—can by any possibility interpose between you and the Source of your life, wisdom, or power. It is all "hidden with Christ [the innermost Christ or Spirit of your being] in God" (Col. 3:3). Nothing but your own ignorance of how to receive, or your willfulness, can hinder your having unlimited supply.

No matter how sick or weak or inefficient you *seem* to be, take your eyes and thoughts right off the seeming and turn them within to the central fountain there and say calmly, quietly, but with steadfast assurance: *This appearance of weakness is false; God, manifest as life, wisdom, and power, is now flowing into my entire being and out through me to the external.* You will soon see a marvelous change wrought in yourself by the realization that this spoken word will bring to you.

You do not change God's attitude toward you one iota by either importuning or affirming. You only change your attitude toward Him. By thus affirming, you put yourself in harmony with divine law, which is always working toward your good and never toward your harm or punishment.

Third: *I am Spirit, perfect, holy, harmonious. Nothing can hurt me or make me sick or afraid, for Spirit is God, and God cannot be sick or hurt or afraid. I manifest my real Self through this body now.*

Fourth: *God works in me to will and to do whatever He wishes me to do, and He cannot fail.*

Our affirming His mind working both to will and to do makes us will only the good, and He, the very Father in us, does the works, hence there can be no failure. Whatever we fully commit to the Father to do and affirm is done, we shall see accomplished.

These, then, are the four comprehensive affirmations:

God is life, love, intelligence, substance, omnipotence, omniscience, omnipresence.

I am a child or manifestation of God, and every moment His life, love, wisdom, power flow into and through me. I am one with God and am governed by His law.

I am Spirit, perfect, holy, harmonious. Nothing can hurt me or make me sick or afraid, for Spirit is God, and God cannot be sick or hurt or afraid. I manifest my real Self through this body now.

God works in me to will and to do whatever He wishes me to do, and He cannot fail.

Commit these affirmations to memory so that you can repeat them in the silence of your own mind in any place and at any time. Strangely will they act to deliver you out of the greatest external distresses, places where no human help avails. It is as though the moment you assert emphatically your oneness with God the Father, there is instantly set into motion all the power of Omnipotent Love to rush to your rescue. And when it has undertaken to work for you, you can cease from external ways and means and boldly claim: *It is done; I have the desires of my heart.*

"You open your hand,
    satisfying the desire of every living
        thing."

—Psalm 145:16

In reality, God is forever in process of movement within us, that He may manifest Himself (All-Good) more fully through us. Our affirming, backed by faith, is the link that connects our conscious human need with His power and supply.

They who have claimed their birthright by thus calmly affirming their oneness with God know how free they can be from human planning and effort, after they have called into operation this marvelous power of affirmation. This power has healed the sick, brought joy in place of mourning, literally opened prison doors and bidden the prisoner go free without the claimants calling for human assistance.

Understand, it is not necessarily the using of just this form of words that has availed in each individual case. It is the denying of apparent evil, and in spite of all contrary evidence, the affirming of good to be all there is, affirming oneness with God's omnipotent power to accomplish, even when there were no visible signs of His being present, that has wrought the deliverance. In one case within my knowledge, just simply claiming *God is your defense and deliverance* for a man who had for five years been an exile from home and country (through a series of deceptions and machinations that for depth and subtlety were unparalleled), opened all the doors wide and restored the man to his family within a month, without any further human effort on the part of himself or his friends, and this, after five years of the most strenuous human efforts of lawyers, had failed utterly to bring the truth to light or to release the prisoner.

Some minds are so constituted that they get better results from repeated use of denials; others, from using denials less and affirmations more.

No definite rules can be laid down as to which will work most effectually in each individual case to eradicate apparent evil and bring the good into manifestation, but some little hint that may be helpful can be given.

Denials have an erasive or dissolving tendency. Affirmations build up and give strength and courage and power. People who remember vividly and are inclined to dwell in their thoughts on the pains, sorrows, and troubles of the past or present need to deny a great deal; for denials cleanse the mind and blot out of memory all seeming evil and unhappiness so that they become as a faraway dream. Again, denials are particularly useful to those who are hard or intolerant, or aggressively sinful; to those who, as a result of success, have become overconfident, thinking the human is sufficient in itself for all things; to the selfish and to any who do not scruple to harm others.

Affirmations should be used by the timid and by those who have a feeling of their own inefficiency, those who stand in fear of other minds, those who "give in" easily, those who are subject to anxiety or doubt, and those who are in positions of responsibility. People who are in any way negative or passive need to use affirmations more; the ones who are self-confident or unforgiving, need denials more.

Deny the appearance of evil; affirm good. Deny weakness; affirm strength. Deny any undesirable condition and affirm the good you desire. This is what Jesus meant when He said, "Whatever you ask for in prayer, believe [or claim and affirm] that you have received it, and it will be yours" (Mk. 11:24). This is what is meant by the promise: "Every place that the sole of your foot will tread upon [or that you stand squarely or firmly upon] I have given to you" (Josh. 1:3).

Practice these denials and affirmations silently in the street, in the car, when you are wakeful during the night, anywhere, everywhere, and they will give you a new, and to you, a strange mastery over external things and over yourself. If there comes a moment when you are in doubt as to what to do, stand still and affirm: *God in me is infinite wisdom; I know just what to do.* "For I will give you words and a wisdom that none of your opponents will be able to withstand or contradict" (Lk. 21:15). Do not get flustered or anxious but depend fully and trustingly on your principle, and you will be surprised at the sudden inspiration that will come to you as the mode of procedure.

So always this principle will work in the solution of all life's problems—I care not what the form of detail is—to free us, God's children, from all undesirable conditions and to bring good into our lives, if we will take up the simple rules and use them faithfully, until they lead us into such realization of our Godhood that we need no longer consciously depend on them.

Study Guide

Bible—Mark 11:24; Luke 21:15

1. Most people seek a higher knowledge of spiritual things because of their _____.

2. To speak an affirmation is to _____
   _____.

3. Four great affirmations are: (1)_____
   _____, (2) _____
   _____,
   (3)_____,
   (4) _____
   _____.

4. It is helpful to commit favorite denials and affirmations to memory so that they will ____
   _____.

5. Denials have an erasive, cleansing tendency; affirmations _____
   _____.

FAITH

Sixth Lesson

"Truly I tell you, if you say to this mountain, 'Be taken up and thrown into the sea,' and if you do not doubt in your heart, but believe that what you say will come to pass, it will be done for you."
—Mark 11:23

Science was faith once.
—Lowell

The word *faith* is one that has generally been thought to denote a simple form of belief based mostly on ignorance and superstition. It is a word that has drawn forth something akin to scorn from so-called "thinking people"—the people who have believed that intellectual attainment is the highest form of knowledge to be reached. "Blind faith" they have disdainfully chosen to call it—fit only for ministers, women, and children, but not a practical thing on which to establish the everyday business affairs of life.

Some have prided themselves on having outgrown the swaddling clothes of this blind, unreasoning faith, and having grown to the point, as they say, where they have faith only in that which can be seen, or intellectually explained.

71

The writer of The Epistle to the Hebrews, obviously a most intellectual man and a learned theologian, before writing at length on the nature of faith and the marvelous results attending it, tried to put into a few words a condensed definition of faith: "Faith is the assurance of things hoped for, the conviction of things not seen" (Heb. 11:1).

In other words, faith takes right hold of the substance of the things desired and brings into the world of evidence the things that before were not seen. Further speaking of faith, the writer said, "What is seen was made from things that are not visible" (Heb. 11:3). In some way, then, we understand that whatever we want is in this surrounding invisible substance, and faith is the power that can bring it out into actuality to us.

After having cited innumerable instances of marvelous things brought to pass in the lives of men, not by their work or efforts, but by faith, the Epistle says: "And what more should I say? For time would fail me to tell of Gideon, Barak, Samson, Jephthah, of David and Samuel and the prophets— who through faith conquered kingdoms, administered justice, obtained promises, shut the mouths of lions, quenched raging fire, escaped the edge of the sword, won strength out of weakness, became mighty in war, put foreign armies to flight. Women received their dead by resurrection" (Heb. 11:32-35).

Do you want any more power or any greater thing than is here mentioned—power to conquer kingdoms, to shut the mouths of lions, quench fire, turn to flight whole armies, raise the dead to life again? Even if your desires exceed this, you need not despair or hesitate to claim their fulfillment, for One greater than you, One who knew whereof He spoke, said, "All things can be done for the one who believes" (Mk. 9:23).

Until very recently, whenever anyone has spoken of faith as the one power that can move mountains, we have always felt a sort of hopeless discouragement. While we have believed that God holds all good things in His hand, and is willing to be prevailed upon to dole them out according to our faith, yet how could we, even by straining every nerve of our being toward faith, be sure that we had sufficient to please Him? For does it not say, "Without faith it is impossible to please God" (Heb. 11:6)?

From the moment we began to ask, we began to question our ability to reach God's standard of faith on which hung our fate. We also began to question whether, after all, there is any such power in faith to prevail with the Giver of "every perfect gift" (Jas. 1:17) so as to draw out of Him something that He had never let us have before.

Viewing faith in this light, there is not much wonder that logical minds have looked on it as a sort of will-o'-the-wisp, not a thing from which any real, definite results could ever be obtained—not a thing that the business world could rest upon.

There is a blind faith, to be sure. (Someone has truthfully said that blind faith is better than none at all; for, if held to, it will get its eyes open after a time.) But there is also an understanding faith. Blind faith is an instinctive trust in a power higher than ourselves. Understanding faith is based on immutable principle.

Faith does not depend on physical facts or on the evidence of the senses because it is born of intuition, or the Spirit of Truth ever living at the center of our being. Its action is infinitely higher than that of reason. It is founded on *Truth*; while as you remember from a former lesson, reasoning or intellectual argument is founded on evidence of the senses and is not reliable.

Intuition is the open end, within one's own being, of the invisible channel ever connecting each individual with God. Faith is, as it were, a ray of light shot out from the central sun—God—one end of which ray comes into your being and mine through the open door of intuition. With our consciousness, we perceive the ray of light, and though intellect cannot grasp it or give the why or wherefore thereof, yet we instinctively feel that the other end of the ray opens out into all there is of God (Good). This is "blind faith." It is based on Truth, but a Truth of which everyone is not at the time conscious. Even this kind of faith will, if persisted in, bring results.

What is understanding faith? There are some things that God has so indissolubly joined together that it is impossible for even Him to put them asunder. They are bound together by fixed, immutable laws; if we have one of them, we must have the other.

This is illustrated by the laws of geometry. For instance, the sum of the angles of a triangle is equal to two right angles. No matter how large or small the triangle, no matter whether it is made on the mountaintop or leagues under the sea, if we are asked the sum of its angles, we can unhesitatingly answer, without waiting an instant to count or reckon this particular triangle, that it is just two right angles. This is absolutely certain. It is certain even before the triangle is drawn by visible lines; we can know it beforehand because it is based on unchangeable laws, on the truth or reality of the thing. It was true just as much before anyone recognized it as it is today. Our knowing it or not knowing it does not change the truth. Only in proportion as we come to know it as an eternally true fact, can we be benefitted by it.

It is also a simple fact that one plus one equals two; it is an eternal truth. You cannot put one and one together without two resulting. You may believe it or not; that does not alter the truth. But unless you do put the one and one together, you do not produce the two, for each is eternally dependent on the other.

The mental and spiritual world or realms are governed by laws that are just as real and unfailing as the laws that govern the natural world. Certain conditions of mind are so connected with certain results that the two are inseparable. If we have the one, we must have the other, as surely as the night follows the day—not because we believe some wise person's testimony that such is the case, not even because the voice of intuition tells us that it is so, but because the whole matter is based on laws that can neither fail nor be broken.

When we know something of these laws, we can know positively beforehand just what results will follow certain mental states.

God, the one creative cause of all things, is Spirit, invisible as we have learned. God is the sum total of all good. There is no good that you can desire in your life that, at its center, is not God. God is the substance of all things—the real thing within every visible form of good.

God, the invisible substance out of which all visible things are formed, is all around us waiting to come forth into manifestation.

This good substance all about us is unlimited and is itself the supply of every demand that can be made, of every need that exists in the visible or natural world.

One of the unerring Truths in the Universe (by "Universe," I mean the spiritual and natural worlds combined) is that there is already provided a lavish abundance for every human want. In other words, the supply of every good always awaits the demand. Another Truth is that the demand must be made before the supply can come forth to fill it. To recognize these two statements of Truth and to affirm them are the whole secret of understanding faith—faith based on principle.

Let us square this by the definition of faith, given earlier in the lesson: "Faith is the assurance of things hoped for, the conviction of things not seen." Faith takes hold of the substance of the thing hoped for and brings into evidence, or visibility, the things not seen.

What are usually called the promises of God are certain eternal, unchangeable Truths that are true whether they are found in the Bible or in the almanac. They are unvarying statements of Truth that cannot be altered. A promise, according to *Webster*, is a something sent beforehand to indicate that something unseen is at hand. It is a declaration that gives the person to whom it is made the right to expect and claim the performance of the act.

The Nazarene recognized the unchangeable Truth that, in the unseen, the supply of every want awaits demand. When he said, "Ask and you will receive" (Jn. 16:24), he was simply stating an unalterable Truth. He knew that the instant we ask or desire (for asking is desire expressed), we touch a secret spring which starts on its way toward us the good we want. He knew that there need not be any coaxing or pleading about it, that our asking is simply our complying with an unfailing law that is bound to work; there is no escape from it. Asking and receiving are the two ends of the same thing. We cannot have one without the other.

Asking springs from desire to possess some good. What is desire? Desire in the heart is always God tapping at the door of your consciousness with His infinite supply—a supply that is forever useless unless there be demand for it. "Before they call I will answer" (Is. 65:24). Before you are ever conscious of any lack, of any desire for more happiness, or for fullness of joy, the great Father-Mother heart has desired them for you. It is He in you desiring them that you feel, and think it is only yourself (separate from Him) desiring them. With God, the desire to give and giving are one and the same thing. Someone has said, "Desire for anything is the thing itself in incipiency"; that is, the thing you desire is not only for you but has already been started toward you out of the heart of God; it is the first approach of the thing itself striking you that makes you desire it or even think of it at all.

The only way God has of letting us know of His infinite supply and His desire to make it ours is for Him to push gently on the divine spark living within each one of us. He wants you to be a strong, self-sufficient man or woman, to have more power and dominion over all before you; so He quietly and silently pushes a little more of Himself, His desire, into the center of your being. He enlarges, so to speak, your real Self, and at once you become conscious of new desire to be bigger, grander, stronger. If He had not pushed at the center of your being first, you would never have thought of new desires but would have remained perfectly content as you were.

You think that you want better health, more love, a brighter, more cheerful home all of your very own; in short, you want less evil (or no evil) and more good in your life. This is only God pushing at the inner door of your being, as if He were saying, "My child, let Me in; I want to give you all good, that you may be more comfortable and happy." "My servants shall eat ... my servants shall drink ... my servants shall rejoice ... my servants shall sing for gladness of heart .... They shall build houses and inhabit them" (Is. 65:13-14, 21).

Remember this: Desire in the heart for anything is God's sure promise sent beforehand to indicate that it is yours already in the limitless realm of supply, and whatever you want you can have for the taking.

Taking is simply recognizing the law of supply and demand (even if you cannot see a sign of the supply any more than Elijah did when he had affirmed for rain, and not a cloud even so big as a man's hand was for a long time to be seen). Affirm your possession of the good that you desire; have faith in it, because you are working with divine law and cannot fail; do not be argued off your basic principle by anyone; and sooner will the heavens fall than that you fail to get that which you desire.

"Whatever you ask for in prayer, believe that you have received it, and it will be yours" (Mk. 11:24).

Knowing the law of abundant supply and the Truth that supply always precedes the demand, demand simply being the call that brings the supply into sight; knowing that all desire in the heart for any good is really God's desire in us and for us, how shall we obtain the fulfillment of our every desire, and that right speedily?

> "Take delight in the Lord,
>   and he will give you the desires of
>   your heart."
>   —Psalm 37:4

Take right hold of God with an unwavering faith. Begin and continue to rejoice and thank Him that you have (not *will* have) the desires of your heart, never losing sight of the fact that the desire is the thing itself in incipiency. If the good were not already yours in the invisible realm of supply, you could not, by any possibility, desire it.

Someone asks: "Suppose I desire my neighbor's wife or his property, is that desire born of God? And can I see it fulfilled by affirming that it is mine?"

You do not and cannot, by any possibility, desire that which *belongs* to another. You do not desire your neighbor's wife. You desire the love that seems to you to be represented by your neighbor's wife. You desire something to fill your heart's craving for love. Affirm that there is for you a rightful and an overflowing supply, and claim its manifestation. It will surely come, and your so-called desire to possess your neighbor's wife will suddenly disappear.

So you do not in reality desire anything that belongs to your neighbor. You want the equivalent of that for which his possessions stand. You want your own. There is today an unlimited supply of All-Good provided in the unseen for every human being. No man need have less that another may have more. Your very own awaits you. Your understanding faith or trust is the power that will bring it to you.

Emerson said that the man who knows the law "is sure that his welfare is dear to the heart of being .... He believes that he cannot escape from his good."

Knowing divine law and obeying it, we can forever rest from all anxiety, all fear, for "you open your hand, satisfying the desire of every living thing" (Ps. 145:16).

Study Guide

Bible—Proverbs 29:25; Matthew 9:29, 21:22; Mark 11:22; Luke 8:25, 17:5

1. "Faith is the _____
   _____" (Heb. 11:1).

2. There is a difference between blind faith and understanding faith. Blind faith is an instinctive belief in a higher power; understanding faith is based on _____
   _____.

3. Faith is born on intuition. Intuition is the open end, within one's own being, of the _____
   _____.

4. We cannot want too much from God. Desire in the heart for anything is God's _____
   _____.

5. We cannot really desire something that belongs to someone else. It is the _____
   of what the possessions stand for that we really desire.

DEFINITION OF TERMS:
CHEMICALIZATION, PERSONALITY, AND INDIVIDUALITY

Seventh Lesson

One of the greatest beauties of the Sermon on the Mount is the childlike simplicity of its language. Every child, every grown person, be he ever so uneducated, if he can read at all can understand it. Not a word in it requires the use of a dictionary; not a sentence in it that does not tell the way so plainly that "no traveler, not even fools, shall go astray" (Is. 35:8). And yet the Nazarene was the fullest, most complete manifestation of the one Mind that has ever lived; that is to say, more of the wisdom that is God came forth through him into visibility than through anyone else who has ever lived. The more any person manifests the true wisdom, which is God, the more simple are his ways of thinking and acting, the more simple are the words through which he expresses his ideas. The greater the truth to be expressed, the more simply can it (and should it) be clothed.

Emerson said, "Converse with a mind that is grandly simple, and all literature [high sounding sentences to convey ideas] looks like wordcatching."

In the metaphysical literature of today, a good many terms are used that are very confusing to

85

those who have not taken a consecutive course of lessons on the subject. It seems to me wise to give here a clear, simple explanation of three words frequently used, so that even the most unlearned may read understandingly.

One term often used and not always clearly understood is *chemicalization.*[1]

Did you ever put soda into sour milk, cider, or other acid fluid and witness the agitation or excited action that takes place? One of the substances neutralizes the other, and something better results from the action.

This is a good illustration of what takes place sometimes in the minds and bodies of people. Suppose a man has lived in wrong thought and molded his body by wrong thought for years, until, as you might say, he has become solidified in that wrong belief. You introduce the Truth to him by strong denials and affirmations as has been taught. The very newness of it (and because it is Truth) creates in the first few days: new hope, new joy, and health. After a little time a sort of mental ferment

1. All editions of *Lessons in Truth* since 1942, with the exception of the 1967, 1971, and 1972 editions, did not include this material on *chemicalization.* It had been thought of as too negative and confusing. We are returning it with all its nineteenth-century flavor because many people experience this phenomenon (by whatever name it is called) and would benefit by reading about it. In the original manuscript, Dr. Cady also included a section on *thought transference,* which we have chosen to leave out because it required considerable rewriting and was not a crucial concept.

or agitation takes place. One is apt to feel very nervous and seared way down in the depths of himself. If he has ever been sick, he will begin to feel the old diseases; if he has been morally bad, the old desires and habits will take possession of him with new force; if he has been holding denials and affirmations about business affairs until they have looked hopeful, all at once they collapse and seem darker and more hopeless than ever. All the new beliefs that lifted him into a new world for a few days seem failures, and he seems on the very verge of breaking up generally.

What has happened? Why, simply this. There has been a clash between the old condition—which was based on falsehood, fear, and wrong ways of thinking—and the new thought or Truth entering into you. The old mortal is kicking vigorously against the Truth. You have a feeling of discouragement or of fear, a feeling such as one would have if caught at something disreputable. Do not be frightened. That which you feel is, on the spiritual plane, a similar excitement and agitation to that which was seen in the chemical action between the alkali and acid on the material plane. And *something higher and better always results.*

This agitation does not always take place with everyone but is most apt to occur with those who have been most fixed and (as it were) solidified in the old beliefs. Such people break up with more resistance. Those who are not very settled in their convictions are more malleable mentally and physically, are not so apt to chemicalize. Vigorous use of denials are also more apt to produce chemicalization than is the use of affirmations. There is always less resistance by the mind when it is gently led into the Truth than when its errors are directly and vigorously combated. Should you find yourself in this state of internal aggravation, you need only affirm: *There is nothing to fear, absolutely nothing to fear. Perfect Love reigns and all is good. Peace be still, and so on,* and very soon the brighter conditions will appear, and you will find yourself on a much higher plane than you have ever been before.

Do not be afraid of this word (or the condition) *chemicalization*—as many have been—for truly, there *is* nothing to fear in it.

The words *personality* and *individuality* present distinct meanings to the trained mind, but by the untrained mind, they are often used interchangeably and apart from their real meanings.[2]

Personality applies to the human part of you— the person, the external. It belongs to the region governed by the intellect. Your personality may be agreeable or disagreeable to others. When you say

2. Today *individuality* and *personality* continue to be used interchangeably in common usage. As with the term *denial,* it is difficult to glean one meaning from a word when it already has another, virtually opposite, meaning in place. Perhaps it may be advisable to use *God Self* instead of *individuality.*

that you dislike anyone, you mean that you dislike his personality—that exterior something that presents itself from the outside. It is the outer changeable man, in contradistinction to the inner or real man.

Individuality is the term used to denote the *real* man. The more God comes into visibility through a person, the more individualized he becomes. By this, I do not mean that one's individuality is greater when one is more religious. Remember, God is wisdom, intelligence, love, power. The more pronounced the manner in which any one of these qualities—or all of them—comes forth into visibility through a man, the greater his individuality.

Emerson was a man of large individuality, but retiring personality. He was grandly simple. He was of a shrinking, retiring nature (or personality). But just in proportion as the human side of him was willing to retire and be thought little of, did the immortal, the God in him, shine forth in greater degree.

John the Baptist represents the illumined intellect, the highest development of human consciousness. We may think of him as standing for personality, whereas Jesus typifies the divine Self or individuality. John, recognizing the superiority of Jesus, said, "He must increase, but I must decrease" (Jn. 3:30).

One's individuality is that part of one that never

changes its identity. It is the God Self. One's personality may become like that of others with whom one associates. Individuality never changes.

Do not confound the terms. One may have an aggressive, pronounced personality, or external man, which will, for a time, fight its way through obstacles and gain its point. But a pronounced individuality never battles; it is never puffed up; it is never governed by likes and dislikes and never causes them in others; it is God come forth in greater degree through a man, and all mere personality instinctively bends the knee before it in recognition of its superiority.

We cultivate individuality by listening to the "still small voice" (1 Kings 19:12 KJV) down deep within us, and boldly following it, even if it does make us different from others, as it surely will. We cultivate personality, in which live pride, fear of criticism, and all manner of selfishness, by listening to the voices outside ourselves and by being governed by selfish motives, instead of by the highest within us. Seek always to cultivate, or to bring into visibility, individuality, not personality. In proportion as one increases, the other must decrease.

Whenever we fear a man, or shrink before him, it is because his personality, being the stronger, overcomes ours. Many timid persons go through life always feeling that they are inefficient, that others are wiser or better than they. They dread to meet a positive, self-possessed person, and when in the presence of such a one, they are laid low, just as a field of tall wheat is after a fierce windstorm has swept across it. They feel as though they would like to get out of sight forever.

All this, dear timid ones, is not because your fellow really is wiser or better than you, but because his personality—the external man—is stronger than yours. You never have a similar feeling in the presence of strong individuality. Individuality in another not only produces in you an admiration for its superiority, but it also gives you, when you are in its presence, a strange new sense of your own inherent possibilities, a sense that is full of exhilaration and comfort and encouragement to you. This is because a pronounced individuality simply means more of God comes forth into visibility through a person, and by some mind process, it has power to call forth more of God through you.

If you want to know how to avoid being overcome and thrown off your feet by the strong personality of others, I will tell you: Always remember that personality is of the human and individuality is of God. Silently affirm your own individuality, your oneness with God and your superiority to personality. Can God fear any person?

If you are naturally inclined to be timid or shrinking, practice of the following will help you overcome it. As you walk down the street and see anyone coming toward you, even a stranger to you, silently affirm such words as: *I am a part of God in visibility; I am one with the Father; this person has no power over me, for I am superior to all personality.* Cultivate this habit of thinking and affirming whenever you approach any person, and you will soon find that no personality, however strong and aggressive, has the power to throw you out of the most perfect poise. You will be Self-possessed because you are God-possessed.

Some years ago I found myself under a sense of bondage to a strong, aggressive personality with whom, externally, I had been quite intimately associated for several months. I seemed to see things through another's eyes, and while I was more than half conscious of this, I could not seem to throw it off. This personality was able, with a very few words, to make me feel as if all that I said or did was a mistake and that I was a most miserable failure. I was always utterly discouraged after being in this presence and felt that I had no ability to accomplish anything.

After vainly trying for weeks to free myself, one day I was walking along the street with a most intense desire and determination to be free. Many times before, I had affirmed that this personality could not affect or overcome me, but with no effect. This day I struck out further and declared (silently of course): *There is no such personality in the universe as this one,* affirming it again and again many times. After a few moments I began to feel wondrously lifted and as if chains were dropping off. Then the voice within me urged me on a step farther to say: *There is no personality in the universe; there is nothing but God.* After a short time spent in vigorously using these words, I seemed to break every fetter. From that day to this, without further effort, I have been as free from any influence of that personality as though it had never existed.

If at any time the lesser affirmation of Truth fails to free you from the influence of other minds, try this more sweeping one: *There is no personality in the universe; there is nothing but God,* and you are bound to be made free.

The more you learn to act from the "still small voice" within you, the stronger and more pronounced will be individuality in you.

If you are inclined to wilt before strong personalities, always remember that God has need of you, through whom, in some special manner, to manifest Himself—some manner for which He cannot use any other organ—what need have you to quail before any person, no matter how important?

However humble your place in life, however unknown to the world you may be, however small your capabilities may seem at present to you, you are just as much a necessity to God in His efforts to get Himself into visibility as is the most brilliant intellect, the most thoroughly cultured person in the world. Remember this always, and act from the highest within you.

Study Guide

Bible—1 Kings 19:12; John 3:30

1. The greater the Truth to be expressed, the
   more _____
   _____.

2. The words *personality* and *individuality*
   present distinct meanings to the trained mind.
   Personality applies to the _____
   part of you; individuality is used to denote
   the _____.

3. In the Bible, John the Baptist stands for_____
   _____; Jesus represents _____.
   What did John the Baptist mean when he
   said, "He must increase, but I must decrease"?
   _____.

4. Always remember that personality is of the
   human, and individuality is of God. To avoid
   being overcome by the strong personality of
   others, affirm your _____
   _____, your own individuality.

5. The more we listen to the " _____ "
   within us, the more pronounced will be
   individuality in us.

SPIRITUAL UNDERSTANDING

Eighth Lesson

"Happy are those who find wisdom,
   and those who get understanding,
for her income is better than silver,
   and her revenue better than gold.
She is more precious than jewels,
   and nothing you desire can compare with
         her.
Long life is in her right hand;
   in her left hand are riches and honor.
Her ways are ways of pleasantness,
   and all her paths are peace.
She is a tree of life to those who lay hold of
         her;
   those who hold her fast are called
         happy....
And whatever else you get, get insight."
                    —Proverbs 3:13-18, 4:7

What is this understanding on the getting of which depends so much? Is it intellectual lore, obtained from delving deep into books of other men's making? Is it knowledge obtained from studying rocks (geology) or stars (astronomy) or even the human body (physiology)? Nay, verily, for when did such knowledge ever ensure life and health and peace, ways of pleasantness, with riches and honor?

Understanding is a spiritual birth, a revelation of God within the heart of man. Jesus touched the root of the matter when, after having asked the apostles a question that was answered variously, according to the intellectual perception of the men, he asked another question to which Peter gave a reply not based on external reasoning, but on intuition. He said to Peter, "Blessed are you, Simon Son of Jonah! For flesh and blood has not revealed this to you, but my Father in heaven" (Mt. 16:17).

You may have an intellectual perception of Truth. You may easily grasp with the mind the statement that God is the giver of all good gifts—life, health, love—just as people have for centuries grasped it. Or you may go further, and intellectually see that God is not only the giver, but the gift itself; that He is life, health, love, in us. But unless Truth is "revealed ... to you" by "my Father in heaven," it is of no practical benefit to you or to anyone else.

This revelation of Truth to the consciousness of a person is spiritual understanding.

You may say to yourself or another may say silently to you, over and over again, that you are well and wise and happy. On the mental plane, a certain "cure" is effected, and for a time you will feel well and wise and happy. This is simply a form of hypnotism, or mind cure. But until, down in the depths of your being, you are *conscious* of your one-ness with the Father, until you know within your-self that the spring of all wisdom and health and joy is within your own being, ready at any moment to leap forth at the call of your need, you will not have spiritual understanding.

All the teachings of Jesus were for the purpose of leading men into this consciousness of their one-ness with the Father. He had to begin at the exter-nal man—because people then as now were living mostly in external things—and teach him to love his enemies, to do good to others, and so forth. These were external steps for them to take—a sort of lopping off of the ends of the branches; but they were steps that led on up to the place of desire and attainment where finally the Master said, "I still have many things to say to you, but you cannot bear them now" (Jn. 16:12).

He told them of the Comforter that was in them, and which would teach them all things, revealing the "depths of God" (1 Cor. 2:10) to them, showing them things to come. In other words, he told them how they might find the king-dom of heaven *within* themselves—the kingdom of love, of power, of life.

The coming of the Comforter to their hearts and lives, giving them power over every form of sin, sickness, sorrow, and over even death itself, is ex-actly what we mean by understanding or realization. The power that this consciousness of the indwelling Father gives is for us today as much as it was for those to whom the Nazarene spoke. Aye, more; for did he not say, "The one who believes in me will also do the works that I do and, in fact, will do greater works than these" (Jn. 14:12)?

All the foregoing lessons have been stepping-stones leading up to the point where man may realize the ever-abiding inner presence of the Most High, God. "Do you not know that your body is a temple of the Holy Spirit within you?" (1 Cor. 6:19)

I cannot reveal God to you. You cannot reveal God to another. If I have learned, I may tell you, and you may tell another how to seek and find God, each within himself. But the new birth into the consciousness of our spiritual faculties and possibilities is indeed like the wind that "blows where it chooses, and you hear the sound of it, but you do not know where it comes from or where it goes. So it is with everyone who is born of the Spirit" (Jn. 3:8). The new birth takes place in the silence, in the invisible.

Intellectual lore can be bought and sold; understanding, or realization, cannot. A man, Simon by name, once attempted to buy the power that spiritual understanding gives from another who possessed it. "But Peter said to him, 'May your silver perish with you, because you thought you could obtain God's gift with money! You have no part or share in this, for your heart is not right before God' " (Acts 8:20-21).

Nor will crying and beseeching bring spiritual understanding. Hundreds of people have tried this method and have not received that for which they earnestly but ignorantly sought. They have not received, because they did not know how to take that which God freely offered. Others have sought with selfish motives this spiritual understanding, or consciousness of the indwelling Father, because of the power it would give them. "You ask and do not receive, because you ask wrongly, in order to spend what you get on your pleasures [or to serve selfish ends]" (Jas. 4:3).

Understanding, or realization of the presence of God within us, is as Jesus said, "the gift of God" (Jn. 4:10). It comes to any and all who learn how to seek it aright. Emerson said, "This energy [consciousness of God in the soul] does not descend into individual life on any other condition than entire possession. It comes to the lowly and simple; it comes to whomsoever will put off what is foreign and proud; it comes as insight; it comes as serenity and grandeur. When we see those whom it inhabits, we are apprised of new degrees of greatness. From that inspiration [consciousness] the man comes back with a changed tone. He does not talk with men with an eye to their opinion. He tries

them.... But the soul that ascends to worship the
great God is plain and true; has no rose color, no
fine friends ... no adventures; does not want admiration; dwells in the hour that now is."

"When you search for me, you will find me; if
you seek me with all your heart" (Jer. 29:13). In
that day when, more than riches and honor and
power and selfish glory, you shall desire spiritual
understanding, in that day will come to you the
revelation of God in you, and you will be conscious
of the indwelling Father, who is life and strength
and power and peace.

One may so desire a partial revelation of God
within himself, a revelation along one line—as, for
instance, that of health—as to seek it with all his
heart. And if he has learned how to take the desired
gift, by uncompromising affirmation that it is his
already, he will get understanding, or realization, of
God as his perfect health. So as with any other
desired gift of God, this is a step in the right direction. It is learning how to take God by faith for
whatever one desires. But in the onward growth,
the time will come to every man when he will hear
the divine voice within him saying, "Come up
higher," and he will pass beyond any merely selfish
desires that are just for his own comfort's sake. He
will desire good that he may have the more to give
out, knowing that as good (God) flows through
him to others, it will make him "every whit whole"

(Jn. 7:23 KJV).

In the beginning of Solomon's reign as king over Israel, the divine Presence appeared to him in a dream at night, saying, "Ask what I should give you" (1 Kings 3:5). And Solomon said, "Give your servant therefore an understanding mind" (1 Kings 3:9)

"It pleased the Lord that Solomon had asked this. God said to him, 'Because you have asked this, and have not asked for yourself long life or riches, or for the life of your enemies, but have asked for yourself understanding to discern what is right, I now do according to your word. Indeed I give you a wise and discerning mind; no one like you has been before you and no one like you shall arise after you. I give you also what you have not asked, both riches and honor all your life; no other king shall compare with you' " (1 Kings 3:10-13).

Thus in losing sight of all worldly goods and chattels, all merely selfish ends, and desiring above all things an understanding heart (or a spiritual consciousness of God within him as wisdom, life, power), Solomon received all the goods or good things included, so that there was none among the kings like unto him in worldly possessions. "Strive first for the kingdom of God [consciousness] and his righteousness, and all these things will be given to you" (Mt. 6:33). "For those who want to save their life [or the things of his life] will lose it, and those who lose their life for my sake [or he that is willing to forget the goods of this life for the truth's sake, choosing before all things the finding of God in his own soul] will find it" (Mt. 16:25).

When you first consciously desire spiritual understanding, you do not attain it at once. You have been living in the external of your being and have believed yourself cut off from God. Your first step after coming to yourself like the prodigal son is to say as he did, "I will get up and go to my father" (Lk. 15:18) to turn your thoughts away from the external seeming toward the central and real; to know intellectually that you are not cut off from God, and that He forever desires to manifest Himself within you as your present deliverance from all suffering and sin. Just as Jesus taught, we begin our journey toward understanding by cutting off the branches of our selfishness. We try to love instead of to hate. Instead of avenging ourselves, we begin to forgive, even if it costs us great mental effort. We begin to deny envy, jealousy, anger, sickness, and all imperfection, and to affirm love, peace, and health.

Begin with the words of Truth that you have learned and which perhaps you have as yet only comprehended with the intellect. You must be willing to take the very first light you receive and use it faithfully, earnestly, to help both yourself and others. Sometimes you will be almost overcome by questions and doubts arising in your own mind when you are looking in vain for results. But you must with effort pass the place of doubt; and some day, in the fullness of God's time, while you are using the words of Truth, they will suddenly be illumined and become to you the Living Word within you—"the true light, which enlightens everyone, was coming into the world" (Jn. 1:9). You will no longer dwell in darkness, for the light will be within your own heart, and the word will be made flesh to you; that is, you will be conscious of a new and diviner life in your body, and a new and diviner love for all people, a new and diviner power to accomplish.

This is spiritual understanding. This is a flash of the Most High within your consciousness. "Everything old has passed away; see, everything has become new!" (2 Cor. 5:17) This will be the time when you will not talk with men with an eye to their opinion. This is when you will suddenly become plain and true, when you will cease to desire admiration, when all words of congratulation from others on your success will fill you with an inexpressible sense of humility, when all mere compliments will be to you as "a noisy gong or a clanging cymbal" (1 Cor. 13:1). Truly, from that inspiration, a man comes back with a changed tone!

With spiritual understanding comes new light on the Scriptures. The very Spirit of Truth, which has come to abide with you forever in your consciousness, takes the deep things of God and reveals them to you. You will no longer run to and fro, seeking teachers or healers and rely solely on them for guidance. You know that the living light, the living word within you, will "guide you into all the truth" (Jn. 16:13).

What we need to do is to seek the revelation of the living Christ within our own being, each for himself, knowing that only this divinity come forth can make us powerful and happy.

Every person in his heart desires, though he may not yet quite know it, this new birth into a higher life, into spiritual consciousness. Everyone wants more power, more good, more joy. And though, to the unawakened mind, it may seem that it is more money as money, or more goods that he wants, it is, nevertheless, more of good (God) that he craves, for all good is God.

Many today are conscious that the inner hunger cannot be satisfied with worldly goods and are with all earnestness seeking spiritual understanding, or consciousness, of an immanent God. They have been seeking long, with a great desire of unselfishness and a feeling that when they have truly found God, they will begin to do for others. Faithful service for others hastens the day-dawning for us. The gifts of God are not given in reward for faithful service, as a fond mother gives cake to her child for being good; nevertheless they are a reward, inasmuch as service is one of the steps that lead up to the place where all the fullness of God awaits men. And while spiritual understanding is in reality a "gift of God," it comes to us more or less quickly in proportion as we use the light that we already have.

I believe that too much introspection, too much of what people usually call "spiritual seeking," is detrimental rather than helpful to the end desired—spiritual growth. Spiritual seeking is a sort of spiritual selfishness, paradoxical as this may seem. From the beginning to the end, Jesus taught the giving of what one possesses to him who has none.

"Is not this the fast that I choose:" said the Spirit of God through the prophet Isaiah, "to loose the bonds of injustice, to undo the thongs of the yoke, to let the oppressed go free ...? Is it not to share your bread with the hungry, and bring the homeless poor into your house; when you see the naked, to cover them ...? Then your light shall break forth like the dawn, and your healing shall spring up quickly .... Then you shall call, and the Lord will answer ... Here I am....

"If you offer your food to the hungry and satisfy the needs of the afflicted, then your light shall rise in the darkness and your gloom be like the noonday. The Lord will guide you continually, and satisfy your needs in parched places, and make your bones strong; and you shall be like a watered garden, like a spring of water whose waters never fail" (Is. 58:6-11).

Stagnation is death. A pool cannot be kept clean and sweet and renewed unless there is an outlet as well as an inlet. It is our business to keep the outlet open and God's business to keep the stream flowing in and through us. Unless you use for the service of others what God has already given to you, you will find it a long, weary road to spiritual understanding.

We cry out and strain every nerve to obtain full understanding, just as sometimes we have heard earnest people, but people wholly ignorant of divine laws, beseech God for the full baptism of "the Holy Spirit" (Lk. 3:16) as in the day of Pentecost. Jesus said, "I still have many things to say to you, but you cannot bear them now" (Jn. 16:12). We grow by using for others the light and knowledge we have. We expand, as we go on step-by-step in spiritual insight, until in the fullness of time—which means when we have grown spiritually to the place where God sees that we are able to bear the many things—we receive the desire of our hearts, understanding.

Seek your own Lord. Take the light as it is revealed to you, and use it for others, and prove for yourself whether there be Truth in this prophecy of Isaiah, that "then your light shall rise in the darkness and your gloom be like the noonday" (Is. 58:10) and "then your light shall break forth like the dawn, and your healing shall spring up quickly" (Is. 58:8).

Study Guide

Bible—Matthew 5:16; Mark 7:14; Luke 15:18;
John 14:1, 26; Colossians 2:2; 1 John 5:20

1. Spiritual understanding differs from intellectual knowledge. Intellectual lore can be
   bought and sold; understanding, or realization
   cannot, for it is a _____
   _____.

2. One of our first steps to take toward gaining
   spiritual understanding is to say, as the prodigal son did, " _____
   _____"; to know that you are
   not intellectually cut off from God.

3. We cannot reveal God to one another. We
   must each find God _____.

4. With spiritual understanding comes new light
   on the _____.

5. Too much "spiritual seeking" is _____
   _____to spiritual growth.

THE SECRET PLACE OF THE MOST HIGH

Ninth Lesson

There is nothing the human heart so longs for, so cries out after, as to know God, "whom to know aright is life eternal."

With a restlessness that is pitiful to see, people are ever shifting from one thing to another, always hoping to find rest and satisfaction in some anticipated accomplishment or possession. Men fancy that they want houses and lands, great learning or power. They pursue these things and gain them only to find themselves still restless, still unsatisfied.

At the great heart of humanity there is a deep and awful homesickness that never has been and never can be satisfied with anything less than a clear, vivid consciousness of the indwelling presence of God, our Father. In all ages, earnest men and women who have recognized this inner hunger as the heart's cry after God, have left seeking after things and have sought, by devoted worship and by service to others, to enter into this consciousness, but few have succeeded in reaching the promised place where their "joy" is "complete" (Jn. 16:24). Others have hoped and feared alternately; they have tried, with the best knowledge they possessed, to "work out" their "own salvation" (Phil. 2:12), not

111

yet having learned that there must be an *in*working as well as an *out*working. "By grace [or free gift] you have been saved through faith, and this is not your own doing [nor of any human working]; it is the gift of God—not the results of works, so that no one may boast" (Eph. 2:8-9).

To him who "dwelleth in the secret place of the most High," there is promised immunity from "the snare of the fowler" and "the deadly pestilence," from "the terror by night" and "the arrow that flieth by day" (Ps 91:1, 3, 5 KJV); and even immunity from *fear* of these things. Oh, the awfully paralyzing effect of fear and evil! It makes us helpless as babes. It makes us ants, whereas we might be giants were we only free from it. It is at the root of all our failures, of nearly all sickness, poverty, and distress. But we have the promise of deliverance from even the fear and evil when we are in the "secret place." "Thou shalt not be afraid for the terror by night" (Ps. 91:5 KJV), and so forth.

> "For he will hide me in his shelter
>   in the day of trouble;
>   he will conceal me under the cover of his tent."
>   —Psalm 27:5

> "In the shelter of your presence you hide them
>   from human plots;
>   you hold them safe under your shelter

from contentious tongues."

—Psalm 31:20

The secret place! Why called a *secret* place? What is it? Where may we find it? How abide in it?

It is a secret place because it is a place of meeting between the Christ at the center of your being and your consciousness—a hidden place into which no outside person can either induct you or enter himself. We must drop the idea that this place of realization of our divinity can be given to us by any human being. No one can come into it from the outside. Hundreds of earnest persons are seeking, night and day, to get this inner revealing. They run from teacher to teacher, many of them making the most frantic efforts to meet the financial obligations thus incurred.

You may study with human teachers and from man-made books until doomsday; you may get all the theological lore of the ages; you may understand intellectually all the statements of Truth, and be able to prate healing formulas as glibly as oil flows, but until there is a definite inner revealing of the reality of an indwelling Christ through whom and by whom come life, health, peace, power, *all* things—aye, who *is* all things—you have not yet found "the friendship of the Lord" (Ps. 25:14).

In order to gain this knowledge—this consciousness of God within themselves—many are willing (and wisely so, for this is greater than all other knowledge) to spend all they possess. Even Paul, after twenty-five years of service and of most marvelous preaching, said: "I regard everything as loss because of the surpassing value of knowing Christ Jesus my Lord.... I regard them as rubbish, in order that I may gain Christ [or the consciousness of his divine Self]" (Phil. 3:8).

Beloved, that which you so earnestly desire will never be found by your seeking it through the mental side alone, any more than it has heretofore been found through the emotional side alone. Intuition and intellect are meant to travel together, intuition always holding the reins to guide intellect. "Come now, and let us reason together, saith the Lord" (Is. 1:18 KJV). If you have been thus far on the way cultivating and enlarging only the mental side of Truth, as probably is the case, you need, in order to come into the fullness of understanding, to let the mental, the reasoning side rest awhile. "Become like children" (Mt. 18:3), and learning how to be still, listen to that which the Father will say to you through the intuitional part of your being. The light that you so crave will come out of the deep silence and become manifest to you from within yourself, if you will but keep still and look for it from that source.

And conscious knowledge of an indwelling God, which we so crave, is that of which Paul wrote to the Colossians, as "the mystery that has been hidden throughout the ages and generations but has now been revealed to his saints.... Christ in you, the hope of glory" (Col. 1:26-27). "The secret place of the most High" (Ps. 91:1 KJV), where each one of us may dwell and be safe from all harm or fear of evil, is the point of mystical union between man and Spirit (or God in us), wherein we no longer believe, but know, that God in Christ abides always at the center of our being as our perfect health, deliverance, prosperity, power, ready to come forth into manifestation at any moment we claim it. We know it. We *know* it. We feel our oneness with the Father, and we manifest this oneness.

To possess the secret of anything gives one power over it. This personal, conscious knowledge of the Father in us is the secret that is the key to all power. What we want is the revelation to us of this marvelous "secret." What will give it to us—who can give it to us except Him, the "Spirit of truth who comes from the Father" (Jn. 15:26)? Surely none other. That which God would say to you and do through you is a great secret that no man on the face of the earth knows, or ever will know, except yourself as it is revealed to you by the Spirit that is in you. The secret that He tells me is not revealed to you, nor yours to me; but each man must, after all is said and done, deal directly with the Father through the Son within himself.

Secrets are not told upon the housetop; nor is it possible to pass this, the greatest of secrets, from one to another. God, the creator of our being, must Himself whisper it to each man living in the very innermost of himself. "To everyone who conquers [or is consciously in process of overcoming] I will give some of the hidden manna, and I will give a white stone [or a mind like a clean white tablet], and on the white stone is written a new name that no one knows except the one who receives it" (Rev. 2:17). It is so secret that it cannot even be put into human language or repeated by human lips.

What you want today and what I want is that the words that we have learned to say as Truth be made alive to us. We want a revelation of God in us as life, to be made to our own personal consciousness as health. We no longer care to have somebody just tell us the words from the outside. We want a revelation of God as love within us, so that our whole being will be filled and thrilled with love—a love that will not have to be pumped up by a determined effort because we know that it is right to love and wrong not to love, but a love that will flow with the spontaneity and fullness of an artesian well, because it is so full at the bottom that it *must* flow out.

What we want today is a revelation to our consciousness of God within us as omnipotent power so that we can, by a word—or a look—"accomplish that which I purpose, and succeed in the thing for which I sent it" (Is. 55:11). We want the manifestation to us of the Father in us so that we can know Him personally. We want to be conscious of God working in us "both to will and to work" (Phil. 2:13) so that we may "work out" our "salvation" (Phil. 2:12). We have been learning how to do the outworking but have now come to a point where we must learn more of how to place ourselves in an attitude where we can each be conscious of the divine inner working.

Mary talked with the risen Jesus, supposing that He was the gardener, until suddenly, as He spoke her name, there flashed into her consciousness a ray of pure intelligence, and in an instant the revelation of His identity was made to her.

According to the same sacred history, Thomas Didymus had walked daily for three years with the most wonderful teacher of spiritual things that has ever lived. He had watched this teacher's life and had been partaker of his very presence, physical and mental. He had had just what you and I have thus far received of mental training and external teaching. But there came a time when there was an inner revealing that made him exclaim, "My Lord and my God!" (Jn. 20:28) The secret name, which no other man could know for him, had that moment been given to him. There had come, in the twinkling of an eye, the manifestation to his consciousness of the Father in him as his Lord and his God. No longer simply our Father and our Lord, but my Lord and my God—my divine Self revealed to me personally.

Is not this that which you are craving?

Each man must come to a time when he no longer seeks external helps, when he knows that the inner revelation of "my Lord and my God" to his consciousness can come to him only through an indwelling power that has been there all the time, waiting with infinite longing and patience to reveal the Father to the child.

This revelation will never come through the intellect of man to the consciousness, but must ever come through the intuitional to the intellect as a manifestation of Spirit to man. "Those who are unspiritual do not receive [or impart] the gifts of God's Spirit, for they are foolishness to them, and they are unable to understand them because they are spiritually discerned" (1 Cor. 2:14), and they must be spiritually imparted.

In our eagerness, we have waited upon every source that we could reach for the light that we want. Because we have not known how to wait upon Spirit within us for the desired revelation, we have run to and fro. Let no one misunderstand me in what I say about withdrawing himself from teachers. Teachers are good and are necessary, up to a certain point. "How are they to call on one in whom they have not believed? And how are they to believe in one of whom they have never heard? And how are they to hear without someone to proclaim him?" (Rom. 10:14)

Books and lectures are good, teachers are good, but you must learn for yourself that Christ, the Son of God, lives in you, that He within you is your light and life and all. When you have once grasped this beyond a doubt with the intellect, you cease looking to teachers to bring you spiritual insight. That Christ lives in you, Spirit itself must reveal to you. Teachers talk about the light, but the light itself must flash into the darkness before you can see the light.

Had the Master remained with the disciples, I doubt whether they would ever have gotten beyond hanging on his words and following in the footsteps of his personality.

Jesus knew that his treatments for spiritual illumination, given to his disciples from his recognition of Truth, would act in them as a seed thought, but he also knew that each man must for himself wait upon God for the inner illumination which is lasting and real. God alone can whisper the secret to each one separately.

The enduement of power was not to come to them by the spoken word through another personality, not even through that of Jesus, with his great spiritual power and discernment. It was to come from "on high" (Is. 32:15) to each individual consciousness. It was the "promise of the Father, which ... ye have heard of me" (Acts 1:4 KJV). He had merely told them about it but had no power to give it to them.

So to each of us this spiritual illumination that we are crying out after, this enduement of power for which we are willing to sell all that we have, must come from "on high," that is, to the consciousness from the Spirit within our being. This is the secret that the Father longs with an infinite yearning to reveal to each individual. It is because of the Father's desire within us to show us the secret that we desire the revelation. It is the purpose for which we came into the world—that we might grow step-by-step, as we are doing, to the place where we could bear to have the secret of His inner abiding revealed to us.

Do not be confused by seeming contradictions in the lessons. I have said heretofore that too much introspection is not good. I repeat it, for there are those who, in earnest desire to know God, are always seeking light for themselves but neglect to use that which they already have to help others.

There must be an equal conscious receiving from the Father and giving out to the world, a perfect equilibrium between the inflowing and the outgiving, to keep perfect harmony. We must each learn how to wait renewedly upon God for the infilling and then go and give out to every creature that which we have received, as Spirit leads us to give, either in preaching, teaching, or silently living the Truth. That which fills us will radiate from us without effort right in the place in life where we stand.

In nearly all teaching of Truth from the purely mental side, there is much said about the working out of our salvation by the holding of right thoughts, by denials and affirmations. This is all good. But there is another side that we need to know a little more about. We must learn how to be still and let Spirit, the I AM, work in us, that we may indeed be made "a new creation" (Gal. 6:15), that we may have the mind of Christ in all things.

When you have learned how to abandon yourself to infinite Spirit and have seasons of doing this daily, you will be surprised at the marvelous change that will be wrought in you without any conscious effort of your own.

It will search far below your conscious mind and root out things in your nature of which you have scarcely been conscious, simply because they have lain latent there, waiting for something to bring them out. It will work into your consciousness light and life and love and all good, perfectly filling all your lack while you just quietly wait and receive. Of the practical steps in this direction, we will speak in another lesson.

Paul, who had learned this way of faith, this way

of being still and letting the I AM work itself into his conscious mind as the fullness of all his needs, was neither afraid nor ashamed to say:

"For this reason I bow my knees before the Father, from whom every family in heaven and on earth takes its name. I pray that, according to the riches of his glory, he may grant that you may be strengthened in your inner being with power through his Spirit, and that Christ may dwell in your hearts through faith, as you are being rooted and grounded in love. I pray that you may have the power to comprehend, with all the saints, what is the breadth and length and height and depth, and to know the love of Christ that surpasses knowledge, so that you may be filled with all the fullness of God" (Eph. 3:14-19).

And then he gives an ascription: "To him who by the power at work within us is able to accomplish abundantly far more than all we can ask or imagine" (Eph. 3:20).

Study Guide

Bible—Psalms 91:1, 27:5; Matthew 6:6

1. Humanity's greatest desire is to _____
   _____.

2. The "secret place" is _____
   _____.

3. The key to all power is the personal, conscious
   _____.

4. The "white stone" upon which a person's
   spiritual name is written represents _____
   _____.

5. There must be an equal conscious receiving
   from the Father and giving out to the world,
   a perfect equilibrium between the inflowing
   and the outgiving, to keep _____
   _____.

FINDING THE SECRET PLACE

Tenth Lesson

Now to seek the secret place—where to find it—how to abide in it—these are questions that today, more than at any other time in the history of the world, are engaging the hearts of men. More than anything else it is what I want. It is what you want.

All the steps that we are taking by speaking words of Truth and striving to manifest the light that we have already received are carrying us on swiftly to the time when we shall have consciously the perfect mind of Christ, with all the love and beauty and health and power which that implies.

We need not be anxious or in a hurry for the full manifestation. Let us not at any time lose sight of the fact that our desire, great as it is, is only God's desire in us. "No one can come to me, unless drawn by the Father who sent me" (Jn. 6:44). The Father in us desires to reveal to us the secret of His presence, else we had not known any hunger for the secret or for Truth.

"You did not choose me but I chose you. And I appointed you to go and bear fruit" (Jn. 15:16).

Whoever you are that read these words, wherever you stand in the world, be it on the platform preaching the gospel or in the humblest little home seeking Truth, that you may make it manifest in a sweeter, stronger, less selfish life, know once and forever that you are not seeking God, but God is seeking you. Your longing for greater manifestation is the eternal energy that holds the worlds in their orbits, *outpushing* through you to get into fuller manifestation. You need not worry. You need not be anxious. You need not strive—only *let* it. Learn how to let it.

After all our beating about the bush, seeking here and there for our heart's desire, we must come right to Him who is the fulfillment of every desire, who waits to manifest more of Himself to us and through us. If you wanted my love or anything that I am (not that I *have*), you would not go to Tom Jones or to Mary Smith to get it. Either of these persons might tell you that I could and would give myself, but you would have to come directly to me and receive of me that which only I am, because I am it.

In some way, after all our seeking for the light and Truth, we must learn to wait, each one for himself, upon God for this inner revelation of Truth and our oneness with Him.

The light that we want is not some *thing* that God has to give; it is God Himself. God does not give us life or love as a thing. God is life and light and love. More of Himself in our consciousness, then, is what we all want, no matter what other name we may give it.

My enduement of power must come from "on high," from a higher region within myself than my present conscious mind; so must yours. It must be a descent of the Holy (whole, entire, complete) Spirit at the center of your being into your conscious mind. The illumination we want can never come in any other way, nor can the power to make good manifest.

We hear a great deal about "sitting in the silence." To many, it does not mean very much, for they have not yet learned how to "wait ... upon God" (Ps. 62:5 KJV), or to hear any voice except external ones. Noise belongs to the outside world, not to God. God works in the stillness, and we can so wait upon the Father of our being as to be conscious of the still, inner working—conscious of the fulfillment of our desires. "Those who seek the Lord lack no good thing" (Ps. 34:10). "Those who wait for the Lord shall renew their strength" (Is. 40:31).

In one of Edward Everett Hale's stories, he speaks of a little girl who, amidst her play with the butterflies and birds in a country place, used to run into a nearby chapel frequently to pray, and after praying, always remained perfectly still a few minutes. "Waiting," she said, "to see if God wanted to say anything" to her. Children are often nearest the kingdom.

When beginning the practice of sitting in the

silence, do not feel that you must go and sit with some other person. The presence of another personality is apt to distract the mind. Learn first how to commune alone with the Creator of the universe, who is all-companionship. When you are able to withdraw from the outside and be alone with Him, then sitting with others may be profitable to you and to them.

There are those who are quite able to still their minds from all outside thoughts, but who, as soon as they get still, find themselves floating out on the astral or psychic plane where spirits of those departed, appear to them, wanting recognition and communication. Right here is a tremendous temptation. The experience is a new one and is more or less fascinating, but if you want the *highest* that is for you, this should not be for a moment yielded to. If, when you begin to get still you find this taking place, get up resolutely and shake it off. Declare it is not what you want; you want the highest spiritual illumination and will not take any other or be intruded upon. If necessary, in order to free yourself, postpone your sitting until another time, when perhaps you will have no trouble.

The psychic plane is all good upon its own level. But it is not what you are seeking. You want your own Spirit brought forth, in all its glorious fullness and Godlikeness, into manifestation. And if you stop on a lower plane to dabble with things there, it will only retard the day of your own realization and manifestation. Put it down at once and it will soon cease to trouble you.[1]

"Sitting in the silence" is not merely a sort of lazy drifting. It is a passive, but a definite, waiting upon God. When you want to do this, take a time when you are not likely to be disturbed, and when you can, for a little while, lay off all care. Begin your silence by lifting up your heart in prayer to the Father of your being. Do not be afraid that, if you begin to pray, you will be too "orthodox." You are not going to supplicate God, who has already given you "whatever you ask for" (Mk. 11:24). You have already learned that before you call He has sent that which you desire; otherwise, you would not desire it.

You know better than to plead with or to beseech God with an unbelieving prayer. But spending the first few moments of your silence in speaking directly to the Father centers your mind on the Eternal. Many who earnestly try to get still and wait upon God have found that the moment they sit down and close their eyes, their thoughts, instead of being concentrated, are filled with every sort of vain imagination. The most trivial things,

---

1. The preceding two paragraphs had been deleted from recent editions. We have returned them for their superb commentary on the importance of "psychic" phenomena. Beginners on the path should be assured that the experience Cady refers to here is not a common experience and it is not to be feared.

from the fixing of a shoestring to the gossipy conversation of a week ago, chase one another in rapid succession through their minds, and at the end of an hour, the persons have gained nothing. This is to them discouraging.

This is but a natural result of trying not to think at all. Nature abhors a vacuum, and if you make (or try to make) your mind a vacuum, the thought images of others that fill the atmosphere about you will rush in to fill it, leaving you as far away from the consciousness of the divine Presence as ever. You can prevent this by beginning your silence with prayer.

It is always easier for the mind to say realizingly, *"Thy will is being done in me now,"* after having prayed, "Let Thy will be done in me." It is always easier to say with realization, *"God flows through me as life and peace and power,"* after having prayed, "Let Thy life flow through me anew while I wait." Of course prayer does not change God's attitude toward us, but it is easier for the human mind to take several successive steps with firmness and assurance than for it to take one big, bold leap to a point of eminence and hold itself steady there. While you are thus concentrating your thoughts on God, in definite conversation with the author of your being, no outside thought images can possibly rush in to torment or distract you. Your mind, instead of being open toward the external, is closed to it, and open only to God, the source of all the good you desire.

Of course there is to be no set form of words used. But sometimes using words similar to the first few verses of the 103rd Psalm, in the beginning of the silent communion, makes it a matter of face-to-face speaking: "You forgive all my iniquities [or mistakes]; You heal all my diseases; You redeem my life from destruction; and crown me with loving-kindness, now, now, while I wait upon You." Sometimes we may enter into the inner chamber with the words of a familiar hymn:

> Thou art the life within me,
>   O Christ, Thou King of Kings
> Thou art Thyself the answer
>   To all my questionings.

Repeat the words many times, not anxiously or with strained effort, not reaching out and up and away to an outside God; but let the petition be the quiet, earnest uplifting of the heart to a higher something right within itself, even to "the Father ... in me" (Jn. 14:11). Let it be made with the quietness and assurance of a child speaking to his loving father.

Some persons carry in their faces a strained, white look that comes from an abnormal "sitting in the silence," as they term it. It is hard for them to know that God is right here within them, and while in the silence they fall into the way of reaching away out and up after Him. Such are earnest men truly feeling after God if haply they may find Him, when all the time He is near them, even in their very hearts. Do not reach out thus. This is as though a seed were planted in the earth, and just because it recognized a vivifying, life-giving principle in the sun's rays, it did nothing but strain and stretch itself upward and outward to get more of the sun. You can see at a glance that by so doing it would get no solid roots in the earth where God intended them to be. The seed needs to send roots downward while it keeps its face turned toward the sun and lets itself be drawn upward by the sun.

Some of us, in our desire to grow and having recognized the necessity of waiting upon God in the stillness for the vivifying and renewing of life, make the mistake of climbing up and away from our bodies. Such abnormal outstretching and upreaching is neither wise nor profitable. After a little of it, one begins to get cold feet and congested head. While one is thus reaching out, the body is left alone, and it becomes correspondingly weak and negative. This is all wrong. We are not to reach out away from the body even after the Son of righteousness. We are, rather, to be still and let the Son shine on us right where we are. The sun draws the shoot up as fast as it can bear it and be strong. We do not need to grow ourselves, only to let the Son "grow" us.

But we are consciously to let it, not merely to take the attitude of negatively letting it by not opposing it, but to put ourselves consciously where the Son can shine on us and then "be still, and know" (Ps. 46:10) that while we wait there, it is doing the work. While waiting upon God, we should, as much as possible, relax ourselves both mentally and physically. To use a very homely but practical illustration, take much the attitude of the entire being as do the fowl when taking a sunbath in the sand. Yet there is something more than a lax passivity to be maintained through it all. There must be a sort of conscious, active taking of that which God gives freely to us.

Let me see if I can make it plain. First, withdraw yourself bodily and mentally from the outside world. "Go into your room and shut the door [the closet of your being, the very innermost part of yourself]" (Mt. 6:6), by turning your thoughts within. Just say: *You abide within me; You are alive there now; You have all power; You are now the answer to all I desire; You do now radiate Yourself from the center of my being to the circumference, and out into the visible world as the fullness of my desire.* Then be still, absolutely still. Relax every part of your being, and believe that it is being done. The divine substance does flow in at the center and out into the visible world every moment you wait; for it is an immutable law that "everyone who asks receives" (Mt. 7:8). And substance will come forth as the fulfillment of your desire if you expect it to. "According to your faith let it be done to you" (Mt. 9:29).

If you find your mind wandering, bring it right back by saying again: *It is being done; You are working in me; I am receiving that which I desire,* and so forth. Do not look for signs and wonders; but just be still and know that the very thing you want is flowing in and will come forth into manifestation either at once or a little further on.

Go even beyond this and speak words of thanksgiving to this innermost Presence, that it has heard and answered, that it does now come forth into visibility. There is something about the mental act of thanksgiving that seems to carry the human mind far beyond the region of doubt into the clear atmosphere of faith and trust, where "all things are possible" (Mt. 19:26). Even if at first you are not conscious of having received anything from God, do not worry or cease from your thanksgiving. Do not return to the asking, but continue giving thanks that while you waited you did receive and that what you received is now manifest; and believe me, you will soon rejoice and give thanks, not rigidly from a sense of duty, but because of the sure manifest fulfillment of your desire.

Do not let waiting in the silence become a bondage to you. If you find yourself getting into a strained attitude of mind, or "heady," get up and go about some external work for a time. Or, if you find that your mind will wander, do not insist on concentrating; for the moment you get into a rigid mental attitude, you shut off all inflow of the Divine into your consciousness. There must be a sort of relaxed passivity and yet an active taking it by faith. Shall I call it *active passivity?*

Of course, as we go in spiritual understanding and desire, we very soon come to the place where we want more than anything else that the desires of infinite wisdom and love be fulfilled in us. "My thoughts are not your thoughts, nor are your ways my ways, says the Lord. For as the heavens are higher than the earth, so are my ways higher than your ways and my thoughts than your thoughts" (Is. 55:8-9).

Our desires are God's desires, but in a limited degree. We soon throw aside our limitations, our circumscribed desires (as soon, at least, as we see that more of God means more of good and joy and happiness), and with all our hearts, we cry out in the silent sitting: *Fulfill Thy highest thought in me now!* We make ourselves as clay in the potter's hands, willing to be molded anew, to be "transformed into the same image" (2 Cor. 3:18), to be made after the mind of the indwelling Christ.

We repeat from time to time, while waiting, words something like these: *You are now renewing me according to Your highest thought for me; You are radiating Your very Self throughout my entire being, making me like Yourself—for there is nothing else but You, Father, I thank You, I thank You.* Be still, be still while He works. "Not by might, nor by power, but by my spirit, says the Lord of hosts" (Zech. 4:6).

While you thus wait and let Him, He will work marvelous changes in you. You will have a strange new consciousness of serenity and quiet, a feeling that something has been done, that some new power to overcome has come to you. You will be able to say, "The Father and I are one" (Jn. 10:30) with a new meaning, a new sense of reality and awe that will make you feel very still. Oh! how one conscious touch of the Oversoul makes all life seem different! All the hard things become easy; the troublesome things no longer have power to worry; the rasping people and things of the world lose all power to annoy. Why? Because, for the time, we see things from the Christ side of ourselves; we see as He sees. We do not have to deny evil; we know in that moment that it is nothing at all. We no longer rigidly affirm the good from sense of duty, but with delight and spontaneity, because we cannot help it. It is revealed to us as good. Faith has become reality.

Do not be discouraged if you do not at once get conscious results in this silent sitting. Every moment that you wait, Spirit is working to make you a new creation in Christ—a creation possessing consciously His very own qualities and powers. There may be a working for days before you see any change, but it will surely come. You will soon get so that you can go into the silence, into conscious communion with your Lord, at a moment's notice, at any time, in any place.

There is no conflict or inconsistency between this waiting upon God to be made perfect and the way of "speaking the word" out toward the external to make perfection visible. Waiting upon and consciously receiving from the Source only make the outspeaking (the holding of right thoughts and words) easy, instead of laborious. Try it and see.

Clear revelation—the word made alive as Truth to the consciousness—must come to every man who continues to wait upon God. But remember, there are two conditions imposed. You are to wait upon God, not simply to run in and out, but to abide, to dwell "in the secret place of the most High" (Ps. 91:1 KJV).

Of course I do not mean that you are to give all the time to sitting alone in meditation and silence, but that your mind shall be continually in an attitude of waiting upon God, not an attitude of clamoring for things, but of listening for the Father's voice and expecting a manifestation of the Father to your consciousness.

Jesus, our Master in spiritual knowledge and power, had many hours of lone communion with the Father, and his greatest works were done after these. So may we, so must we, commune alone with the Father if we would manifest the Christ. But Jesus did not spend all his time in receiving. He poured forth into everyday use, among the children of men in the ordinary vocations of life, that which he received of the Father. His knowledge of spiritual things was used constantly to uplift and to help other persons. We must do likewise, for newness of life and of revelation flows in the faster as we give out that which we have to help others. "Go, preach .... Heal the sick ... freely ye have received, freely give" (Mt. 10:7-8 KJV), he said. Go manifest the Christ within you, which you have received of the Father. God works in us to will and to do, but we must work out our own salvation.

The second indispensable condition to finding the secret place and abiding in it is "my hope is from him":

> "For God alone my soul waits in silence,
>   for my hope is from him."
>   —Psalm 62:5

"Truly in vain is salvation hoped for from the

hills, and from the multitude of mountains: truly in the Lord our God is the salvation of Israel" (Jer. 3:23 KJV). It is good that a man should both hope and quietly wait for the salvation of the Lord.

Is your hope from Him, or is it from books or teachers or friends or meetings or societies?

"The king of Israel, the Lord, is in your midst" (Zeph. 3:15). Think of it—in the midst of you—at the center of your being this moment while you read these words. Say it, say it, think it, dwell on it, whoever you are, wherever you are! In the midst of you! Then what need for all this running around? What need for all this strained outreaching after Him?

"The Lord, your God, is in your midst [not just God in the midst of others, but in the midst of you, standing right where you are], a warrior who gives victory; he will rejoice over you with gladness, he will renew you in his love; he will exult over you with loud singing" (Zeph. 3:17). You are His love. It is you that He will rejoice in with singing if you will turn away from people to Him within you. His singing and joy will so fill you that your life will be a great thanksgiving.

The Lord is the Lord within our own being. The Lord is the Christ of our own being.

There is one Spirit, one Father of all, in us all, but who manifests uniquely in each of us. Your Lord is He who will deliver you out of all your troubles. Your Lord has no other business but to manifest Himself to you and through you, and so make you mighty with His own mightiness made visible, whole with His health, perfect by showing forth the Christ perfection.

Standing in the place of intellect or conscious mind, we thus look to Spirit. Spirit flows in and illumines intellect making it see its oneness with Spirit; and then we—conscious mind—stand at the center, and, looking from within outward say, "The Father and I are one."

Let all your hope be from your Lord. Let your communion be with Him. Wait upon the inner abiding Christ often, just as you would wait upon any visible teacher. When you are sick "wait thou only upon God" (Ps. 62:5 KJV) as the Most High, rather than upon healers. When you lack wisdom in small or large matters, "wait thou only upon God," and see what marvelous wisdom for action will be given you. When desiring to speak the word that will deliver another from the bondage of sickness or sin or sorrow, "wait thou only upon God" and exactly the right word will be given you, and power will go with it, for it will be alive with the power of Spirit.

Study Guide

Bible—Isaiah 40:31; Psalm 46:10; John 6:44, 16:13

1. To many, "sitting in the silence" does not mean very much, for they have not yet learned

    _____.

2. We can prevent our mind from wandering by beginning our silence with _____

    _____.

3. The mental act of thanksgiving carries the human mind far beyond the region of doubt into the clear atmosphere of _____.

4. There may be a working for days before you see any change come as a result of true prayer, but it will come. What are some of the changes that will come? _____

    _____

5. There are two indispensable conditions of finding the secret place. First, we must wait _____and, secondly, our_____must be from Him.

SPIRITUAL GIFTS

Eleventh Lesson

It is very natural for the human heart first to set out in search of Truth because of the "loaves and the fish" (Mt. 15:36).

Perhaps it is not too much to say that the majority of people first turn to God because of some weakness, some failure, some almost unbearable want in their lives. After having vainly tried in all other ways to overcome or to satisfy the want, they turn in desperation to God.

There is in the heart of even the most depraved human being, though he would not for worlds have others know it, an instinctive feeling that somewhere there is a power that is able to give him just what he wants; that if he could only reach that which to his conception is God, he could prevail on Him to grant the things desired. This feeling is itself God-given. It is the divine Self, though only a spark at the center of the man's being, suggesting to him the true remedy for all his ills.

Especially have people been led to seek Truth for the reward, for "the works themselves" (Jn. 14:11), during the last few years, since they have come to know that God is not only able, but willing, to deliver them from all the burdens of their everyday life. Everyone wants to be free, free, free as the birds of the air—free from sickness, free from suffering,

143

free from bondage, free from poverty, free from all
forms of evil—and he has a right to be; it is a God-
given desire and a God-given right.

Thus far nearly all teaching has limited the manifestation of infinite love to one form—that of healing. Sickness, seemingly incurable disease, and suffering reigned on every side, and every sufferer
wanted to be free. We had not yet known that there
was willingness as there was power—aye, more,
that there was intense desire—on the part of our
Father to give us something more than sweet,
patient submission to suffering.

When first the Truth was taught that the divine
Presence ever lives in man as perfect life and can be
drawn on by our recognition and faith to come
forth into full and abounding health, it attracted
widespread attention, and justly so. Both teachers
and students centered their gaze on this one out-
come of a spiritual life, losing sight of any larger,
fuller, or more complete manifestation of the
indwelling Father. Teachers told all of their pupils
most emphatically that this knowledge of Truth
would enable them to heal, and they devoted all of
their teaching to explanation of the principles and
to giving formulas and other instructions for healing the body. This has brought both disappointment and discouragement to many. Failing to heal,
they have, for the time, abandoned the entire principle. Time has shown that there are larger and

broader views of the Truth about spiritual gifts.

Healing of the body is beautiful and good. Power to heal *is* a divine gift, and as such you are fully justified in seeking it. But God wants to give you infinitely more.

Why should you and I restrict the limitless One to the bestowal of a particular gift, unless, indeed, we be so fairly consumed with an inborn desire for it that we are sure that it is God's highest desire for us? In that case, we shall not have to try to heal. Healing will flow from us wherever we are. Even in a crowd of people, without any effort of our own, the one who *needs* healing will receive it from us; that one will "touch" (Mt. 9:21) us, as did the one woman in all the multitude jostling and crowding against Jesus. Only one *touched* him.

The power to heal the body has heretofore been, as I have already said, set up as a test of one's spiritual understanding. At first, all who come into some knowledge of the Truth do heal more or less; but there comes a time to many when, in their onward growth, they fail to heal.

This has brought great disappointment not unmixed with considerable humiliation. But, my dear friends, do not let such an experience discourage you. It only means that *God is leading you upward into higher things.* Every denial of evil and affirmation of good you have made has served to push you upward. Do not fear or get nervous because you seem to "fail." Failure is often success written with a capital S.

The time has probably come in your spiritual growth when you are no longer to cling to just the one spiritual gift. God's thoughts for you are not as your thoughts for yourself. "For as the heavens are higher than the earth, so are my ways higher than your ways and my thoughts than your thoughts" (Is. 55:9).

Healing is truly a "branch" of "the vine" (Jn. 15:4), but it is not the only branch. There are many branches, all of which are necessary to the perfect vine, which is seeking through you and me to bear much fruit. What God wants is that we shall grow into such conscious oneness with Him, such realization that He who is the substance of all good really abides in us, that "ask for whatever you wish, and it will be done for you" (Jn. 15:7).

If you are faithfully and earnestly living what Truth you know and still find that your power to heal is not so great as it was at first, recognize it as All-Good. Be assured, no matter what anyone else says to you or thinks, that the seeming failure does not mean loss of power. It means that you are to let go of the lesser in order that you may grasp the whole in which the lesser is included. Do not fear for a moment to let go of just this one little branch of divine power; choose rather to have the highest thoughts of Infinite Mind, let them be what they may, fulfilled through you. We need to take our eyes off the ends of the branches, the results, and keep them centered in the vine.

Some are excellent physical healers but it is astonishing how little their other spiritual gifts are developed. At least, it would be astonishing if we did not know that healing is probably their special gift. Divine life flows through them in great abundance because, to them, physical life and health are the highest desire and attainment. Hence they become channels for divine Presence to flow through in that one direction alone. They are chosen vessels for that purpose.

You are a vessel for some purpose. If, when the time comes, you let go cheerfully, without humiliation or shame or sense of failure, your tense, rigid mortal grasp on some particular form of manifestation, such as healing, and "strive for the greater gifts" (1 Cor. 12:31), whatever they may be in your individual case, you will do "works" in the one specific direction that will be simply marvelous in the eyes of men. These works will be done without effort on your part, because they will be God, omnipotent, omniscient, manifesting Himself through you in His own chosen direction.

Paul said: "Now concerning spiritual gifts, brothers and sisters, I do not want you to be uninformed.... There are varieties of gifts, but the same Spirit .... To one is given through the Spirit the utterance of wisdom, and to another the utterance of knowledge according to the same Spirit ... faith ... gifts of healing ... the working of miracles ... prophecy ... discernment of spirits ... various kinds of tongues, to another the interpretation of tongues" (1 Cor. 12:1, 4, 8-10).

Spirit is always and forever the same, one God, one Spirit, but in different forms of manifestation. The gift of healing is no more, no greater, than the gift of prophecy; the gift of prophecy is no greater than faith, for faith (when it is really God's faith manifested through us), even as a grain of mustard seed, shall be able to remove mountains. The working of miracles is no greater than the power to discern spirits (or the thoughts and intents of other men's hearts, which are open always to Spirit). And "greatest of these is love" (1 Cor. 13:13); for "love never ends" (1 Cor. 13:8) to melt down all forms of sin, sorrow, sickness, and trouble. "Love never ends."

"All these are activated by one and the same Spirit, who allots to each one individually just as the Spirit chooses. For just as the body is one and has many members, and all the members of the body, though many, are one body, so it is with Christ.... If the whole body were an eye [or gift of healing], where would the hearing be? If the whole body were hearing, where would the sense of smell be?... The eye cannot say to the hand, 'I have no need of you,' nor again the head to the feet, 'I have no need of you.' But as it is, God arranged the members in the body, each one of them, as he chose" (1 Cor. 12:11-12, 17, 21, 18).

Thus Paul enumerates some of the free "gifts" of the Spirit to those who will not limit the manifestations of the Holy One, but yield themselves to Spirit's desire within them. Why should we so fear to abandon ourselves to the workings of infinite love and wisdom? Why be so afraid to let Him have His own way with us and through us?

Has not the gift of healing, the only gift we have thus far sought, been a good and blessed one, not only to ourselves, but to all with whom we come in contact?

Then why should we fear to wait upon God with a perfect willingness that the Holy Spirit manifest itself through us as it will, knowing that, whatever the manifestation, it will be good—all good to us and to those around us!

Oh, for more men who have the courage to abandon themselves utterly to Infinite Will—men who dare let go every human being for guidance, and seeking the Christ within themselves, let the manifestation be what He wills!

Such courage might possibly mean, and probably would mean at first, a seeming failure, a going down from some apparent success that had been in the past. But the going down would only mean a mighty coming up, a most glorious resurrection of God into visibility through you in His own chosen way, right here and now. The failure, for the time, would only mean a grand, glorious success a little later on.

Do not fear failure, but call failure good, for it really is. Did not Jesus stand as an utter failure, to all appearances, when he stood dumb before Pilate, all his cherished principles come to naught, unable (yes, I say it, *unable* or else not tempted in all points as we are) to deliver himself, or to "demonstrate" over the agonizing circumstances of his position?[1]

But had he not "failed" right at that point, there never would have been the infinitely grander demonstration of the Resurrection a little later on. "Unless a grain of wheat falls into the earth and dies, it remains just a single grain; but if it dies, it bears much fruit" (Jn. 12:24). If you have clung to one spiritual gift because you were taught that, and you begin to fail, believe me, it is only the seeming death, the seeming disappearance, of one gift, in order that out of it may spring many new gifts—brighter, higher, fuller ones, because they are the ones that God has chosen for you.

Your greatest work will be done in your own

1. *Unable* in the sense of being unable to go against God's will. Our personal demonstrations must always be in harmony with and not in resistance to the will of God.

God-appointed channel. If you will let Spirit possess you wholly, if you will to have the highest will done in you and through you continually, you will be quickly moved by it out of your present limitations, which a half success always indicates, into a manifestation as much fuller and more perfect and beautiful as is the new grain than the old seed, which had to fall into the ground and die.

Old ways must die. Failure is only the death of the old that there may be the hundredfold following. If there comes to you a time when you do not demonstrate over sickness, as you did at first, do not think that you need lean on others entirely. It is beautiful and good for another to "heal" you bodily by calling forth universal life through you, but right here there is something higher and better for you.

Spirit, the Holy Spirit, which is God in movement, wants to teach you something, to open a bigger, brighter way to you. This apparent failure is His call to you to arrest your attention and turn you to Him.

> "Agree with God, and be at peace;
>   in this way good will come to you."
>   —Job 22:21

Turn to the divine Presence within yourself. Seek Him. Be still before Him. Wait upon God quietly, earnestly, but constantly and trustingly, for days—

aye weeks, if need be! Let Him work in you, and sooner or later you will spring up into a resurrected life of newness and power that you never before dreamed of.

When these transition periods come, in which God would lead us higher, should we get frightened or discouraged, we only miss the lesson that He would teach and so postpone the day of receiving our own fullest, highest gift. In our ignorance and fear, we are thus hanging on to the old grain of wheat that we can see, not daring to let it go into the ground (of failure) and die (or fail), lest there be no resurrection, no newness of life, nothing bigger and grander to come out of it.

Oh, do not let us longer fear our God, who is all good, and who longs only to make us each one a giant instead of an ant!

What we all need to do above everything else is to cultivate the acquaintance or consciousness of Spirit within ourselves. We must take our attention off results and seek to live the life. Results will be "given to" (Mt. 6:33) us in greater measure when we turn our thoughts less to the "works" and more to embodying the indwelling Christ in our entire being. We have come to a time when there must be less talking about Truth, less treating and being treated merely for the purpose of being delivered from some evil result of wrong living; there must be more living of Truth and teaching others to do so.

There must be more incorporating of Truth in our very flesh and bone.

How are you to do this?

"I am the way, and the truth, and the life" (Jn. 14:6), says the Christ at the center of your being.

"I am the vine, you are the branches. Those who abide [consciously] in me and I in them [in His consciousness], bear much fruit, because apart from me [or severed from me in your consciousness] you can do nothing.... If you abide in me, and my words abide in you, ask for whatever you wish, and it will be done for you" (Jn. 15:5, 7).

I do assure you, as do all teachers, that you can bring good things of whatever kind you desire into your life by holding to them as yours in the invisible until they become manifest. But, beloved, do you not see that your highest, your first—aye, your continual—thought should be to seek the abiding in Him, to seek the knowing as a living reality, not as a finespun theory that He abides in you? After that, ask what you will, be it power to heal, to cast out demons, or even the "greater works" (Jn. 14:12), and "it will be done for you" (Jn. 15:7).

There is one Spirit—"One God and Father of all, who is above all and through all and in all. But each of us was given grace [or free gift] according to the measure of Christ's gift" (Eph. 4:6-7)—in us.

"For this reason I remind you to rekindle the gift of God that is within you" (2 Tim. 1:6).

Do not be afraid, "for God did not give us a spirit of cowardice, but rather a spirit of power and of love and of self-discipline" (2 Tim. 1:7).

It is all one and the same Spirit. To be the greatest success, you do not want my gift, nor do I want yours; each wants his own, such as will fit his size and shape, his capacity and desires, such as not the human mind of us, but the highest in us, shall choose. Seek to be filled with Spirit, to have the reality of things incarnated in larger degree in your consciousness. Spirit will reveal to your understanding your own specific gift, or the manner of God's desired manifestation through you.

Let us not desert our own work, our own God within us, to gaze or pattern after our neighbor. Let us not seek to make his gift ours; let us not criticize his failure to manifest any specific gift. Whenever he "fails," give thanks to God that He is leading him into a higher place, where there can be a fuller and more complete manifestation of the divine Presence through him.

And "I ... beg you to lead a life worthy of the calling to which you have been called, with all humility and gentleness, with patience, bearing with one another in love, making every effort to maintain the unity of the Spirit in the bond of peace" (Eph. 4:1-3).

Study Guide

Bible—Psalms 2:7-8, 37:4; Matthew 7:11; John 4:10; Acts 2:38; Romans 6:23, 12:6; 1 Corinthians 12:1, 4

1. Most people turn to God because of some ___ _____in their lives.

2. The power to heal is a great divine gift, but there are many other spiritual gifts as well. One could be given the gift of _____ _____, while another the gift of_____ _____.

3. Paul said that "there are varieties of gifts, but the same _____."

4. The Truth about an apparent failure is that it is really _____because something higher and better is coming to you.

5. The Holy Spirit is God _____.

UNITY OF THE SPIRIT

Twelfth Lesson

If we did not know it as a living reality that behind all the multitude and variety of human endeavors to bring about the millennium there stands forever the master Mind, which sees the end from the beginning, the master Artist who, through human vessels as His hands, is putting on the picture here a touch of one color and there a touch of another according to the vessel used, we might sometimes be discouraged.

Were it not at times so utterly ridiculous, it would always be pitiful to see the human mind of man trying to limit God to personal comprehension as though the finite ever could completely encompass or comprehend the Infinite. However much any one of us may know of God, there will always be unexplored fields in the realms of expression, and it is evidence of our narrow vision to say: "This is all there is of God."

Suppose that a dozen persons are standing on the dark side of a wall in which are various sized openings. Viewing the scene outside through the opening assigned to him, one sees all there is within a certain radius. He says, "I see the whole world; in it are trees and fields." Another, through a larger opening, has a more extended view; he says, "I see trees and fields and houses; I see the whole world."

The next one, looking through a still larger opening, exclaims: "Oh! You are all wrong! I alone see the whole world; I see trees and fields and houses and rivers and animals."

The fact is, each one looking at the same world sees according to the size of the aperture through which he is looking, and he limits the world to just his own circumscribed view of it. You would say at once that such limitation was only a mark of each man's ignorance and narrowness. Everyone would pity the man who thus displayed—aye, fairly vaunted—his ignorance.

From time immemorial, there have been schisms and divisions among religious sects and denominations. And now with the newer light that we have, even the light of the knowledge of one God immanent in all men, many still cling to external differences, so postponing, instead of hastening, the day of the millennium; at least they postpone it for themselves.

I want, if possible, to help break down the seeming "dividing wall" (Eph. 2:14), even as Christ, the living Christ, does in reality break down or destroy all misunderstanding. I want to help you to see that there is no real wall of difference between all the various sects of the new theology, except such as appear to you because of your circumscribed view. I want you to see, if you do not already, that every time you try to limit God's manifestation of

Himself in any person or through any person, in order to make that manifestation conform to what you see as Truth, you are only crying loudly: "Ho! Everyone, come and view my narrowness and my ignorance!"

I want to stimulate you to lose sight of all differences, all side issues and lesser things, and seek but for one thing—that is the consciousness of the presence of an indwelling God in you and your life. And believe me, just as there is less separation between the spokes of a wheel the nearer they get to the hub, so you will find that the nearer you both come to the perfect Center, which is the Father, the less difference will there be between you and your brother.

The faith healer, he who professes to believe only in what he terms "divine healing" (as though there could be any other healing than divine), differs from the so-called spiritual scientist only in believing that he must ask, seek, knock, importune, before he can receive; while he of the Truth teaching knows that he has already received God's free gift of life and health and all things and that by speaking the word of Truth the gifts are made manifest. Both get like results (God made visible) through faith in the invisible. The mind of the one is lifted to a place of faith by asking or praying; the mind of the other is lifted to a place of faith by speaking words of Truth.

Is there any real difference?

The mental scientist usually scorns to be classed with either of the other two sects. He loudly declares that "all is mind" and that all the God he knows or cares anything about is the invincible, unconquerable *I* within him, which nothing can daunt or overcome.

He talks about conscious mind and subconscious mind, and he fancies that he has something entirely different from and infinitely higher than either of the other sects. He boldly proclaims, "I have Truth; the others are in error, too orthodox," and thus he calls the world's attention to the small size of the aperture through which he is looking at the stupendous whole.

Beloved, as surely as you and I live, it is all one and the same Truth. There may be a distinction, but it is without difference.

The happy person who will from his heart exclaim, "Praise the Lord!" no matter what occurs to him, and who thereby finds that "all things work together for good for those who love God" (Rom. 8:28), is in reality saying the "all is good" of the metaphysician. Each one does simply "in all your ways acknowledge him [or God, Good]" (Prov. 3:6), which is indeed a magical wand, bringing sure deliverance out of any trouble to all who faithfully use it.

The teachings of Spirit are intrinsically the same,

because Spirit is one. I heard an uneducated woman speak in a most orthodox prayer meeting some time ago. She knew no more of religious science than a babe knows of Latin. Her face, however, was radiant with the light of the Christ manifest through her. She told how, five or six years before, she had been earnestly seeking to know more of God (seeking in prayer, as she knew nothing about seeking spiritual light from people), and one day, in all earnestness, she asked that some special word of His will might be given directly to her as a sort of private message. These words flashed into her mind: "If therefore thine eye be single, thy whole body shall be full of light.... No man can serve two masters" (Mt. 6:22, 24 KJV).

She had read these words many times, but that day they were illumined by Spirit; and she saw that to have an eye "single" meant seeing but one power in her life; while she saw two powers (God and devil, good and evil) she was serving two masters. From that day to this, though she had passed through all sorts of troublous circumstances—trials of poverty, illness in family, intemperate husband— she found always the most marvelous, full, and complete deliverance out of them all by resolutely adhering to the "single" eye—seeing God only. She would not look even for a moment at the seeming evil to combat it or rid herself of it, because, as she said, "Lookin' at God with one eye and this evil with the other is bein' double-eyed, and God told me to keep my eye single."

This woman, who had never heard of any science or metaphysical teaching or laws of mind was combating and actually overcoming the tribulations of this world by positively refusing to have anything but a single eye. She had been taught in a single day by infinite Spirit the whole secret of how to banish evil and have only good and joy in her. Isn't it all very simple?

At the center, all is one and the same God forevermore. I believe that the veriest heathen that ever lived, he who worships the golden calf as his highest conception of god, worships God. His mind has not yet expanded to a state where he can grasp any idea of God apart from a visible form, something that he can see with human eyes and handle with fleshly hands. But at heart, he is seeking something higher than his present conscious self to be his deliverance out of evil.

Are you and I, with all our boasted knowledge, doing anything more or different?

The Spirit at the center of even the heathen, who is God's child, is thus seeking, though blindly, its Father-God. Shall anyone dare to say that it will not find that which it seeks—its Father? Shall we not rather say it will find, because of that immutable law that "everyone who searches finds" (Mt. 7:8)?

You have now come to know that, at the center of your being, God (omnipotent power) ever lives. From the nature of your relationship to Him, and by His own immutable laws, you may become conscious of His presence and eternally abide in Him and He in you.

The moment that any man really comes to recognize that which is absolute Truth—namely, that one Spirit, even the Father, being made manifest in the Son, ever lives at the center of all human beings—he will know that he can cease forever from any undue anxiety about bringing others into the same external fold that he is in. If your friend or your son or your husband or your brother does not see Truth as you see it, do not try by repeated external arguments to convert him.

"And I, when I am lifted up from the earth, will draw all people to myself" (Jn. 12:32). That which is needed is not that you (the human, which is so fond of talk and argument) try to lift up your brother. The Holy Spirit, or Christ within him, declares: "And I, when I am lifted up ... will draw all people." You can silently lift up this *I* within the man's own being, and it will draw the man up unto—what? Your teaching? No, unto Christ, the Divine in him.

Keep your own light lifted by living the victorious life of Spirit. And then, remembering that your dear one, as well as yourself, is an incarnation of the

Father, keep him silently committed to the care of his own divine Spirit. You do not know what God wants to do in him; you never can know.

If you fully recognize that the God that dwells in you dwells in all men, you know that each one's own Lord, the Christ within each one, will make no mistake. The greatest help that you can give to any man is to tell him silently, whenever you think of him: *The Holy Spirit lives within you; He cares for you, is working in you that which He would have you do, and is manifesting Himself through you.* Then let him alone. Be at perfect rest about him, and the result will be infinitely better than you could have asked.

Keep ever in mind that each living person in all God's universe is a radiating center of the same perfect One, some radiating more and some less, according to the awakened consciousness of the individual. If you have become conscious of this radiation in yourself, keep your thought centered right there, and the Spirit of the living God will radiate from you in all directions with mighty power, doing without noise or words a great work in lifting others up. If you want to help others who are not yet awakened to this knowledge, center your thoughts on this same idea of them—that they are radiating centers of the All-Perfect. Keep your eye "single" for them, as did the uneducated woman for herself, and Spirit will teach them more in a day than you could in years.

Throughout the ages, man has leaned to the idea of separateness instead of oneness. He has believed himself separate from God and separate from other men. And even in these latter days when we talk so much about oneness, most teachers of metaphysics manage again to separate God's children from Him by saying that while the child may suffer, the Father knows no suffering, nor does He take cognizance of the child's suffering; that we, His children, forever a part of Him, are torn and lacerated, while He, knowing nothing of this, goes on as serenely and indifferently as the full moon sails through the heavens on a winter night.

It is little wonder that many, to whom the first practical lessons in the gospel of the Christ came as liberation and power, should in time of failure and heartache have turned back to the old limited belief of the fatherhood of God.

There is no real reason why we, having come to recognize God as infinite substance, should be by this recognition deprived of the familiar fatherly companionship that in all ages has been so dear to the human heart. There is no necessity for us to separate God as substance and God as tender Father; no reason why we should not, and every reason why we should, have both in one; they are one—God principle outside of us as unchangeable law, God within us as tender, loving Father-Mother, who has compassion for our every sorrow.

There is no reason why, because in our earlier years some of us were forced into the narrow puritanical limits that stood for a religious belief, we should now so exaggerate our freedom as to fancy that we are entirely self-sufficient and shall never again need the sweet, uplifting communion between Father and child. The created, who ever lives, moves, and has his being in his Creator, needs the conscious presence of that Creator, and cannot be entirely happy in knowing God only as cold, unsympathetic principle. Why cannot both conceptions find lodgment in the minds and hearts? Both are true, and both are necessary parts of a whole. The two were made to go together, and in the highest, cannot be separated.

God as the underlying substance of all things, God as principle, is unchanging and does remain forever uncognizant of and unmoved by the changing things of time and sense. It is true that God as principle does not feel pain, is not moved by the cries of children of men for help. It is a grand, stupendous thought that this power is unchanging law, just as unchanging in its control of our affairs as it is in the government of the starry heavens. One is fairly conscious of his entire being expanding into grandeur as he dwells on the thought.

But this is not all, any more than the emotional side is all. True, there is law, but there is gospel also.

Gospel does not make law of no effect; it fulfills law. God is principle, but God is individual also. Principle becomes individualized the moment it comes to dwell in external manifestation in a human body.

Principle does not change because of pity or sympathy, even "as a father has compassion for his children" (Ps. 103:13). The Father in us always moves into helpfulness when called on and trusted. It is as though infinite wisdom and power, which outside are Creator, Upholder, and Principle, become transformed into infinite love, which is Father-Mother, with all the warmth and tender helpfulness that this word implies, when they become focalized, so to speak, within a human body.

I do not at all understand it, but in some way, this indwelling One does move to lift the consciousness of His children up and to place it parallel with God, Principle, Law, so that no longer two are crossed, but the two—aye, the three—the human consciousness, the indwelling individual Father, and the Holy Spirit—are made one. In every life, with our present limited understanding, there come times when the bravest heart goes down, for the moment, under the apparent burdens of life; times when the strongest intellect bends like "a reed shaken by the wind" (Mt. 11:7), when the most self-sufficient mind feels a helplessness that wrings from it a cry for help from "the rock that is higher than I" (Ps. 61:2).

Every metaphysician either has reached, or must in the future reach, this place—the place where God as cold principle alone will not suffice any more than in the past God as personality alone could wholly satisfy. There will come moments when the human heart is so suddenly struck as to paralyze it, and for the moment it is impossible, even with strained effort, to think right thoughts.

At such times there will come but little comfort from the thought: This suffering comes as the result of my wrong thinking; but God, my Father, takes no cognizance of it: I must work it out unaided and alone. Just here we must have, and we do have, the motherhood of God, which is not cold principle any more than your love for your child is cold. I would not make God as principle less, but God as individual more.

The whole business of your Lord (the Father in you) is to care for you, to love you with an everlasting love, to note your slightest cry, and to rescue you.

Then you ask, "Why doesn't He do it?" Because you do not recognize His indwelling and His power, and by resolutely affirming that He does now manifest Himself as your all-sufficiency, call Him forth into visibility.

God (Father-Mother) is a present help in time of

need; but there must be a recognition of His presence, a turning away from human efforts, and an acknowledgment of *God only* (a single eye) before He becomes manifest.

Study Guide

Bible—John 12:32, 17:11; Ephesians 2:14

1. There is no limit to God; however, the manifestation of God in us is limited when we try to _____.

2. To have a "single" eye means seeing God as _____.

3. We should not try to convert others to Truth by repeated external arguments. Our attitude regarding this should be _____ _____.

4. The idea of oneness is important, why?_____ _____ _____ _____

5. God is a present help in our time of need, but there must be a _____, a_____, and an acknowledgment of_____ _____.

A Brief Glossary of Truth Terms

NOTE: The terms *Truth* (capitalized) and *Unity* are used to designate the principles taught by Unity School of Christianity and presented to the public through its literature. The term *Truth* (capitalized) means that which is the fundamental and ultimate reality of anything. Truth may transcend fact. For instance, to a Unity student, a person's illness is fact, not Truth; he believes that the Truth about the person is wholeness; he believes that wholeness is God's will for His children and that wholeness is the fundamental and ultimate reality of each person's being.

Being—God; Deity.

being—finite existence.

consciousness—sum total of inner awareness.

demonstrate—to bring forth; reveal; prove.

demonstration—outward expression; proof.

Divine Mind—God.

manifest—to bring into form; to make evident to the senses; prove; give evidence of.

manifestation—that which has been brought forth as evident to the senses; expression.

meditate—to contemplate or ponder; to dwell in thought.

metaphysics—that division of philosophy that includes the science of being or reality, or the science of the fundamental causes and processes in things.

principle—basic law.

reality—that which is absolute or ultimately true.

realization—clear, vivid knowing; understanding.

the silence—state of stillness, relaxation, and receptivity wherein one may experience the presence of God.

Spirit—God; Deity.

spirit—life; the principle.

spiritual consciousness—inner or intuitive awareness of the things of Spirit.

substance—the spiritual essence out of which all things are made.

Index

abundance, 77

affirmation(s), 59-70, 102, 104, 121, 133-134, 136, 164; for deliverance, 13; for freedom, 92-93; four comprehensive, 62-65; of Elijah, 80; repetition of, 62, 65; specific usefulness of, 67; to overcome timidity, 91-92

All-Good, 30, 39

All-Perfection, 23, 164

anger, to be denied, 53, 104

animal part of man, 2-3

anxiety, 67-68, 82, 125-126, 163

appearance(s), negative, 49; of evil, 51, 63, 68; of weakness, 63

argument, 29, 30, 33, 163

Artist, master, 157

asceticism, 9

ask(ing), 78, 134, 146, 159

aspiration, 59

astronomy, 97

attitude toward God, 64

automatons, 35

beauty, 125

Being, 19; statement of, 17-24

being, 8, 19, 79, 99, 106, 113-116, 120, 127, 130, 133, 139, 152, 163

beseeching, 101, 129

Bible, 77
birth, new, 100, 106; spiritual, 98
birthright, 66
blood, 34
body, 28, 34, 38, 50, 97, 132, 144-145, 167;
    envy of parts of, 54; torturing, 43
bondage, 9, 92, 135, 140, 144; freedom from
    through denial, 54; to false beliefs, 11; to
    the flesh, 2, 4, 7
books, 31, 113, 119, 139
bugaboos, 48, 55
business, 74

Center, perfect, 159
center of being, 79, 113, 115, 127, 139, 143,
    153, 163
channel(s), 37, 108, 151
chemicalization, 86-88
child(ren), 30, 33, 35, 39, 48, 114, 118, 131,
    165
child(ren) of God, 5-6, 52, 63, 65, 69, 162,
    166-167
Christ, gospel of, 165; indwelling, 6, 31, 106,
    113, 115, 118, 135, 137, 139, 152, 159,
    164; mind of, 121, 125; place of meeting,
    113; way of, 13
Christ Spirit, 10
circumstances, 11, 34, 55, 161; can be changed,
    47; controlled by thoughts, 50

clay, 135
closet of our being, 133
comfort, spring of, 4
Comforter, 99
communion, 128, 131, 137, 140, 166
companionship, 128, 165
concentrating, 135
conditions, denial of, 50; troublesome, 47, 59,
    68-69; two, for revelation, 137-138
consciousness, awakened, 164; error, 48;
    human, 2-3, 8, 89, 106, 116, 121, 127,
    135, 137, 154, 167; inner, 12, 74, 98, 113,
    118; new, 136; of indwelling Father, 99,
    101-102, 111, 113, 130, 152, 159; of
    Mary, 117; spiritual, 76, 100, 103, 106
contradictions, seeming, 120
conversation, idle, 8
courage, 11, 67, 149
creations of God, 21
creative cause, 21
creative energy, 17
criticism, fear of, 90
cure, 98

death, power over, 99; seeming 150; unreality of,
    52
decree, 61
deliver(ance), 2, 12-13, 29, 65-66, 104, 112,
    115, 139, 143, 160-162

demand and supply, law of, 60, 77-80

demons, power to cast out, 153

demonstration, 13, 150

denial(s), 43-56, 61, 67, 104, 121, 136; how
    spoken, 55; of fear, 54; of four common
    error thoughts, 52-53; repetition of, 62;
    specific usefulness of, 67

denominations, 158

deprivation, 46

desire(s), 23, 34, 50, 55, 59-61, 65, 68, 76,
    78-81, 99, 102, 106, 108, 114, 120, 125-
    127, 134-135, 144-145, 153

destiny, 4

devil, 63, 161

difference(s), 159-160

digestion, 34

disappointment, 23, 44

disciples, 119

discouragement, 35, 73, 92, 130, 137

disease, 38

dissatisfaction, 59

Divine Mind, 29, 33

divine plan, 50

divine Presence, 144, 151

divine spark, 79

Divine, prompting of within us, 60

divine voice, 102

divinity, 106, 113

doing, 8, 60

dominion, man's, 3, 7, 20-21, 79
doubt, 67-68, 105, 134
dream, 103

education, 19
Emerson, 81, 85, 89, 101
emotional side, 114
enduement of power, 120, 126-127
energy, 126
environment, 11-12
envy, denial of, 55, 104
equilibrium, 120
error, 62, 160
error thoughts, four common, 51-52
escape, 12
establishing the word, 61
evil(s), 36, 51, 61, 63, 66, 68, 79, 112, 115,
    136, 144, 161-162
experience, 35
external, 23, 28, 36, 44, 46, 64-65, 88, 99, 104,
    118, 130, 137, 163
eye, single, 161-162, 164, 169

faculties, spiritual, 100
failure, seeming, 149-151, 154, 165
faith, 66, 71-82, 102, 121-122, 134-136, 144,
    148, 159; blind, 74; understanding,
    74-75
faith healer, 159

false accusation, 10
false beliefs, 5, 11, 62; about God, 48; arise only
        in human mind, 47; can be changed, 47;
        consequence of, 47
Father, access to, 23, 115; desire of, 120;
        indwelling, 4, 21, 46, 64, 99-100, 101,
        114, 116, 118, 125, 129, 131, 139, 144,
        159, 162-163, 165-168; oneness with,
        51, 65, 99, 115, 136; receiving from,
        120, 138; waiting upon, 127, 137
Father-Mother God, 23, 39, 78, 165-169
fear, 35, 52, 54, 68, 82, 90, 112, 152, 154
forgiveness, 10-11, 104
formulas, healing, 113
fountain(head), 10, 23, 37, 54-55, 63
fowl, 133
freedom, 55, 69, 144, 166
fulfillment, 50, 126-127, 134-135, 167

geology, 97
geometry, 75
giant, 112, 152
gift(s), 102; spiritual, 143-154; varieties of,
        147-148
giving, 78, 120
God, access to, 31; as central sun, 74; as creative
        cause, 21, 76, 116; as invincible, 160; as
        love, 18, 62-63, 65, 89, 116, 126; as
        Omnipotence, 19, 36, 62-63, 65, 116, 147,

163; as perfect health, 102; as personal being, 17, 18, 22; as power, 19, 89; as principle, 22, 166, 168; as Spirit, 17; as substance, 20, 62-63, 65, 76, 165-166; as total of all good, 45, 50, 76, 106; as wisdom and intelligence, 19, 62-63, 65, 89; attitude unchanged, 64, 130; business of, 108; but one, 18; cannot be sick, hurt, afraid, 64, 166; children of, 5; coming into visibility, 85, 89-91, 93; consciousness of, 113, 163; control of our thoughts, 35; cut off from, 104; deep things of, 99, 106; desire of, 80, 125, 135; displeasure of, 38-39; expression of, 46; gifts of, 107, 150, 159; giver of all good gifts, 98, 130-131, 145; happiness, health, and power from, 54; has need of you, 93; heart of, 78; held by His own laws, 61; how He regards man, 5; human longing to know, 111; immanent, 106, 158; impersonality of, 23; indwelling, 12, 111, 114, 131, 159, 164; infinite supply of, 78; in movement, 151; inner presence of, 101; invisible, 60; law of His being, 38; manifesting Himself through us, 65-66, 104, 115, 154, 158-159; motherhood of, 168; nature of, 44; need not be beseeched, 38, 101; never changes, 39, 162, 166; not an autocrat, 3; oneness with, 63, 65-66, 92, 146, 164; our attempts to limit, 157; our

desire and power to please, 34, 73; our relation to, 37; plans of, 63; pleasing and placating, 43; promises of, 77; pushing on
divine spark, 79; quantity of, made manifest, 62; revelation of, 98, 102, 105-106,
116-117; seeking, 100, 106, 120, 126; standard of faith, 73; submission to, 48; things
joined together by, 75; turning to in desperation, 45, 143; waiting upon, 120-121,
126-127, 129, 133, 137, 140, 149, 151;
works in stillness, 127; wrong thoughts
about, 33-34, 38, 48
Godhood, realization of, 69
God-possessed, 92
good, 19, 36, 38, 55, 61-62, 64, 68, 74, 76, 79-
80, 102, 106, 127, 135-136, 145, 149,
160, 162; absence of, 51; all things working
together for, 11; invisible, 60; God is total
of, 18, 45
gospel, 165-167
grace of God, 112, 153
grain, 150, 152
gratification, 46
growth, 36, 102, 107-108, 120, 132; through
prayer, 51
guidance, 106, 149

Hale, 127
happiness, 54-55, 78, 135

harm, safe from, 115
harmony, 10, 34, 64, 120
healer(s), 106, 140
healing, 144-149, 151, 159
health, 55, 79, 97-99, 102, 104, 113, 115-116,
        125, 140, 144
heart, 35, 79-80, 98, 103, 105, 111, 131-132,
        143, 148, 165
heirs, 5
Holy One, 149
Holy Spirit, 108, 127, 149, 151, 163-164
homesickness, 111
hope, 138, 140
hunger, 23, 106, 111, 125
hymn, 131
hypnotism, 98

I, 21, 23, 28, 160, 163
I AM, 121
ideas, 85
idleness, 8
ignorance, 38, 44, 63, 108, 152, 158-159
illumination, 33, 120, 127, 161
ill will, 53
immunity, 112
imperfection, 104
importuning, 64, 159
individual(ity), 27-28, 36-37, 85-94, 139, 167-
        168

inefficiency, 63, 67, 90
inharmony, 10
inheritance, 6
inlet, 5-6, 108
inner presence, 100
inner working, 111-112, 117
insight, spiritual, 108, 120-121
inspiration, 68
intellect, 3, 5, 28, 30, 32, 38, 88-89, 94, 104,
        114, 118-119, 167
intellectual perception, 33, 71, 98, 100, 113
intelligence, God is, 19; no absence of, 51-52
intolerance, 67
introspection, 107, 120
intuition, 74, 98, 114, 117-118
invisible, 72, 100, 153, 159
Israel, Children of, 2

jealousy, denial of, 53, 104
Jericho, walls of, 13
Jesus, as healer, 145; as seeming failure, 150;
        communed with Father, 138; purpose of
        teachings of, 99; question based on intu-
        ition, 98; talked with Mary, 117; teachings
        of, 104, 107; treatments for illumination,
        119; typifies divine Self or individuality, 89
John the Baptist, 89
joy, 66, 78, 106, 111, 135, 139, 162; spring of,
        5, 99

kingdom of heaven, 30, 99

knowledge, of spiritual things, 30, 59, 113-114,
    138, 162; of the Father, 115, 158; source
    of, 19; spiritual, 7

lack, 78, 121

law, 33, 76, 81, 162, 166; divine, 3, 7, 38, 61,
    63-64, 80, 82, 108, 167; of demand and
    supply, 60, 78, 80, 133-134

lesson, 152

let, 126, 133, 136

life, 98-99, 102, 113, 116, 119, 121, 126, 144,
    151-152, 167; higher, 106; new, 10, 105,
    138, 152; no absence of, 52; of God,
    37-38; of Spirit, 10, 163; renewing of, 132;
    Source of, 63

light, 32, 74, 104-109, 114, 118, 120-121,
    125-126, 158, 161, 163

limitation(s), 23, 135, 151, 158-159, 165

Lord, 139-140, 164, 168

love, 7-8, 10, 79, 81, 98-99, 104, 116, 121,
    125-126, 135, 139, 144, 148-149, 167;
    God is, 18, 50, 126; law of 3; new, 105; of
    parents, 36, 167; universal, 22

man, composite, 28; deals directly with Father,
    115; highest manifestation, 20; inner, 89;
    intellectual, 33, 46, 118; outer, 88-89, 99;

purpose of, 120; servant or child of God, 5;
   ultimate aim of, 12
manhood, spiritual, 36
manifestation(s), 20, 22, 27, 50, 63-64, 76, 81,
   85, 114-115, 117-118, 125-126, 134,
   137-139, 144, 147, 149, 151, 153-154,
   158-159, 163, 167-169
Mary, 117
mathematics, 75
mechanical steps to spiritual life, 55-56, 60
meditation, 7, 137
meekness, 10
memory, 65, 67
mental scientist, 160
mental side, 114, 121
metaphysics, 31, 85, 160, 162, 165, 168
method of studying, 1
millennium, 157-158
Mind, universal, 27, 29, 32, 36-37, 85, 157
mind(s), carnal, 29, 46; cleansing of, 51; conditions of, 76; exhilaration of, 34; human, 2,
   10, 12, 21, 28, 36-37, 67, 127, 130, 134,
   157, 159, 160, 167-168; Infinite, 146-147;
   influence of, 93; laws of, 162; of Christ,
   121, 125, 135; of God, 64; spiritualizing,
   43; training of, 62; unawakened, 106
mind cure, 98
miracles, 148
money, 106

Most High, 100, 105, 111-122, 137, 140
motherhood of God, 168
music, 7

name, secret, 117
Nazarene, 9, 13, 44, 77, 85, 100
need, call of, 99
negation, 53-54
neighbor's wife, 81
nervousness, 9
new birth, 100, 106
new creation, 137

ocean, 20
offspring, of God, 22
old age, unreality of, 52
omnipotence, 19, 36, 62-63, 65, 116, 147
omnipresence, 19, 51, 62-63, 65
omniscience, 19, 62-63, 65, 147
oneness with God, 50-51, 63, 65, 66, 91-92, 99,
    115, 164, 167
opinion, 31-33, 105
order, of divine law, 3
orthodox, 160-161
others, service for, 106, 108, 111, 120, 138, 164
outlet, 5, 108
outreaching, 132
outspeaking, 137
outworking, 111-112, 117, 120-121

overconfidence, 67
oversensitiveness, 9
Oversoul, 136

pain, unreality of, 52
passivity, 133, 135
patience, 32, 118
Paul, 33, 114, 121-122, 147, 149
peace, 10, 97, 102, 104, 113
Pentecost, 108
people, two classes of, 29
personality, 11, 22, 85-94, 119, 128, 168
Pharisees, 33
physiology, 97
Pilate, 10, 150
poise, 92
possessions, 44, 81, 103, 106, 111
poverty, 52, 112, 144, 161
power, 106, 125, 136, 143-144, 167-168;
     adverse 63; desire for, 111; enduement
     of, 120, 127; God is, 19; indwelling,
     118; in word of faith, 61; key to, 115;
     kingdom of, 99; like that of Jesus, 46;
     lives within us, 13; new, 105; of faith,
     72; of Omnipotent Love, 65; of Spirit,
     140, 164; omnipotent, 116; secret of, 7;
     Source of, 63, 113; spring of, 4; that spiri-
     tual understanding gives, 100; the one, 51,
     161; through affirmations, 67; to bring

invisible good into expression, 60; to heal, 145; weakened through negation, 54
practice the presence of God, 7
prayer, 51, 127, 129, 161
preaching, 121, 125
Presence, 61, 103, 134, 144
pride, 90
Principle, 22, 166-168
principle(s), 68, 80, 150
prison(er), 66-67
prodigal son, 104
projections of God, 22
promises, 77
prophecy, 148
prosperity, 115
psychic plane, 128
purpose, 147, 152

quiet, 7, 136

radiating, 37, 39, 55, 121, 164
reality, 153
realization, 13, 99-102, 130, 146
reasoning, 98, 114
receiving, 78, 101, 120, 134, 138
recognition, 144, 164-165, 168
Red Sea, 4
relationship, 22
relaxing, 133

religious science, 161
repetition of affirmations and denials, 62, 65,
    131
reservoir, 37
responsibility, 68
restlessness, 111
results, 7, 34, 76, 105, 137, 152, 159,
    164
resurrection, 150, 152
revealing, 99, 113, 117
revelation, 30, 32, 102, 106, 115-118, 120,
    126, 137-138
reward(s), 106-107, 143
rheumatism, 35
roots, 132
rules, 31, 69

salvation, 31, 111, 117, 121, 138
satiation, 44
Scriptures,105
secret, 116, 119-120, 125, 162
secret place of Most High, 111-122; finding,
    125-140
secret spring, 78
sects, 158
seed, 132, 151
seeking, spiritual, 107, 113-114
seeking God, 100-102, 106, 108, 126, 151,
    159, 162

Self, divine, 46, 89, 114, 118, 143; ignorance of, 33-34; real, 46, 64, 79; spiritual, 3, 28

self, human, 46, 162

selfish(ness), 67, 90, 101-104, 107, 126

self-reliance, 35

sense, man, 2

senses, 29, 33, 74

separateness, 28, 159, 165

serenity, 136

Sermon on the Mount, 85

servants of the Most High, 5

service, 106, 108

shoulders, stooped, 35

sick(ness), 44, 52, 63, 65, 99, 104, 112, 140, 143-144, 151, 161

signs and wonders, 134

silence, 65, 100, 114, 127-132, 135, 137

simplicity, 85

sin, 99, 140

slaves of circumstance, 5

Solomon, 103

Son, 115, 119, 132-133

soul, 28

Source, 23, 63, 137

Spirit, 17-18, 21, 27-28, 33, 37, 64, 76, 120-122, 136, 139-140, 147-148, 151-153, 160-164; as Divine Mind, 29; fulfillment of our desires, 60; manifestation of, 118; of Truth, 19, 31-32, 74, 105, 115; union

      with man, 115
spirit, 33
spirits, power to discern, 148
spiritual scientist, 159
stagnation, 37, 108
"still small voice," 90, 93
still(ness), 9, 114, 121-122, 127, 132
straining, 131-132, 135, 139
strength, 67, 102
submission, 48, 144
substance, 20, 52, 60, 72, 76, 133, 146, 165
suffer(ing), 2, 11, 47, 165, 168; freedom from,
      3, 143-144
sun, 38, 49, 63, 132
supplication, 129
supply, 12, 60, 63, 66, 76-77, 79-81

taking, 80, 101, 133
talk, 10
teacher(s), 19, 45, 106, 113, 117-119, 139-140,
      144, 153
temporal things, 36
thanksgiving, 80, 134, 139
theology, 158
thinking, 27-39, 130, 168; false, 34, 38
Thomas Didymus, 117
thought(s), at random, 34; centered on God, 8,
      164; control bodies and circumstances,
      50; negative, 34-35; of Divine Mind, 33;

of fear and grief, 35; right, 7, 34, 121, 137, 168; seed, 119; turn away from external, 104; wrong, 27, 34-35, 168
thought images, 129-130
time, 7; fullness of, 6, 105, 108
timidity, 67, 90-91
transition periods, 152
treating, 152
trust, 81, 134
Truth, 6-7, 31-34, 45, 49, 74, 93, 98, 104-105, 108, 114, 116, 121, 137, 144-146, 152-153, 159-160, 163; knowledge of, 29-30, 144; of Being, 10; repetition of, 62; revelation of, 98; search for, 6, 125-126, 143; statement(s) of, 9, 77, 104, 113, 125
truth(s), 75

understanding, 29, 86, 114, 167; spiritual, 3, 30-31, 97-109, 135
unforgiveness, 11
unity of the Spirit, 157-169
Universe, 77, 164
unknown, power to meet, 8
unselfishness, 106

vacuum, 130
varieties of gifts, 147, 154
vessel(s), 147, 157
vine, 146-147

vision, 157-158
vivifying, 132

water, 20
weakness, 68
whole, 20, 23, 54, 102, 127, 140, 146, 160, 166
will, free, 28; infinite, 149; of God, 64, 161
willfulness, 38, 63
wisdom, 19, 135, 140, 149; of God, 38, 85,
        167; Source of, 63, 99
withdrawal, 133
word(s), 85, 104-105, 116, 119, 161; form of,
        66, 131; speaking, 61, 64, 125, 137, 140,
        159
works, 143, 147, 152-153
worship, 111, 162

yield, to Spirit, 149
young people, 44

About the Author

Dr. Harriet Emilie Cady was born on September 12, 1848, on a farm near Dryden, New York. Very little is known about her personal life. She never married, and she started her professional life as a teacher in a little school in Dryden. Dr. Cady left to study homeopathic medicine and probably was one of the first woman doctors in New York.

Early in her career as a physician, she discovered that her patients' ills were too deep for outer remedies to cure. In accord with the tenets of homeopathy, she began treating her patients as spiritual beings, helping them find within themselves the source of health for mind and body. She became convinced that God was always the healer.

Dr. Cady's openness to Truth ideas led her to become a student of Emma Curtis Hopkins, the New Thought pioneer. She wrote a booklet called *Finding the Christ in Ourselves*, which fell in the hands of Myrtle Fillmore, who co-founded Unity along with her husband Charles. They were so impressed with the author's spiritual discernment, they wrote Dr. Cady and invited her to write for them.

The first of several articles in *Unity Magazine* appeared in January 1892 ("Neither Do I Condemn Thee"). Her articles met with instant approval of the readers, many of whom asked her to

193

write a simple course of lessons on the principles of divine healing. At first she was doubtful, then she consented. From the appearance of the first lesson "Statement of Being" (*Unity Magazine,* October 1894), these lessons met with an extraordinary response. Continued demand for extra copies of the magazines in which the lessons were printed led Charles Fillmore to have them reprinted in three booklets, four lessons in each booklet. In 1903 *Lessons in Truth* came out in book format and has since been translated into eleven languages and sold over a million and a half copies.

An impressively tall woman with strong features and a hearty voice, Dr. Cady did not meet the Fillmores until 1927 when they visited her in New York. As part of her belief in not emphasizing the personality, she never visited Unity Village. She died in her home in January 1941 at the age of 92.

H. Emilie Cady was a woman who proved God within her life. The fruits of her life, her writings, are so full of light and life that they continue to inspire readers today. Certainly, the works of Dr. Cady are of the caliber of a spiritual classic, some of the very best the movement of metaphysical Christianity has yet produced.

Printed U.S.A   114-1509-20M-6-95